ON BEHALF OF THE ENVIRONMENT
PEDAGOGIES OF UNREST

SPECTOR BOOKS

CONTENTS

On Behalf of the Environment
Pedagogies of Unrest

Bauhaus Lab 2024

EXPERIMENTS IN ENVIRONMENTAL DESIGN: A BAUHAUS LEGACY?

A volume of essays by the Swiss architect and theorist Claude Schnaidt titled *Umweltbürger und Umweltmacher* is published by the Verlag der Kunst Dresden in 1982, a time in which the architecture scene in the GDR is embroiled in combative discussions about the concept of 'complex environmental design'. This debate had its roots in the transformation processes of a socialistic modern age, including socio-economic shifts, new intellectual horizons, ideological manoeuvres and realignments in the disciplines of architecture and city planning. The book contains essays from various periods of Claude Schnaidt's oeuvre; thoughts on the Bauhaus, on Hannes Meyer and his critical reception in the post-war modern era are recurring themes. In this context, Schnaidt also examines the concept of functionalism and grapples with questions about the future training of architects. After studying architecture in Geneva, Schnaidt had, after all, gained a second diploma at the Hochschule für Gestaltung Ulm (HfG Ulm) before becoming a lecturer there, teaching industrial building. At this point in time, Schnaidt already showed an interest in the work of Hannes Meyer, the second director of the Bauhaus; the first edition of Meyer's writings (Arthur Niggli Verlag, 1965) would not have been published without Schnaidt's backing. Walter Gropius's postscript, added to this by the publisher, testifies to the intense ideological controversies that accompanied the reception of the Bauhaus, especially as regards Hannes Meyer, during post-war modernity.

The final section of *Umweltbürger und Umweltmacher* focuses on the Bauhaus's reception in France and on the attempts to initiate a transition from product design to environmental design at the HfG Ulm and closes with an essay on the Institut de l'Environnement in Paris, of which Claude Schnaidt became director in 1968 and which closed down after just 18 months.[1] The Bauhaus Lab 2024, titled *On behalf of the environment: pedagogies of unrest* focuses on this educational experiment in which the concept of environment became a code for a radical rethinking of the architect's field of knowledge and practice, trialling new ways of connecting research and design. The book to hand documents the findings of this three-month multidisciplinary research project.

For the Bauhaus Dessau Foundation, the analysis of this French institution's history was of interest in several respects. Firstly, the HfG Ulm and its successor institution in Paris saw themselves as heirs to the Bauhaus, even though their references to the avantgarde school were now influenced by the social and geopolitical contexts of the 1960s. International student protests, the oil crisis and the associated awareness of the finite nature of natural resources, and the formation of a global environmental movement are just a few facets of the crisis scenarios that formed the backdrop for the formation of the Institut de l'Environnement, providing an important source of inspiration for its energy and creativity. In this framework, there was also a critical revision of the social role of architecture and design and the way in which it was taught. The complicity of these disciplines in capitalistic mass production and the exploitation of natural resources led to debates about whether design was even possible under the conditions of late capitalism. Tomás Maldonado, former principal of the HfG Ulm, took a clear position on this in the

1970 essay *Umwelt und Revolte. Zur Dialektik des Entwerfens im Spätkapitalismus.*[2] In this context, the debate about the Bauhaus's legacy also became a way of defining one's position on the respective forms of modernism. The break with what was described as 'Bauhaus machine age modernism', its aesthetics and politics was most clearly manifested in the counterculture movements of the west coast of North America, which Greg Castillo and others called 'hippie modernism'.[3]

Secondly, debates about the concept of environment also played a role in the GDR from the 1970s on. The housing construction programmes initiated as a national policy measure opened up the architecture community's field of practice. In the 1970s, architectural theorist Bruno Flierl introduced the term *komplexe Umweltgestaltung*[4] (complex environmental design) to the architectural discourse of the GDR. This conceived of the built environment as a system comprising diverse elements—from landscape, transport, infrastructure and cultural and educational institutions to supply—which needed to be organised and configured. This also entailed changes to the job profiles of architects and planners. Without going into the conflict between the architects' plans and the planned economy restrictions and government guidelines that shaped the development of large-scale housebuilding projects, with this concept of the environment designers in East Germany too pursued a systematic approach, moving away from product design and towards the environmental project. In doing so, they found ideas, inspiration and interexchange in the newspapers, magazines and congresses of their West German and international peers. Claude Schnaidt, who as a Marxist and Swiss national was active in both systems despite the Iron Curtain, soon contributed to debates in the journal *Form+Zweck* and participated in the international Bauhaus colloquia organised by the Hochschule für Architektur und Bauwesen Weimar. The first colloquium titled 'Die progressiven Ideen des Dessauer Bauhauses und ihre Bedeutung für die sozialistische Entwicklung von Städtebau und Architektur sowie für die industrielle Formgestaltung in der DDR' (The progressive ideas of the Bauhaus Dessau and their significance for the socialistic development of city planning, architecture and industrial design in the GDR) coincided with the re-opening of the Bauhaus Building in Dessau. The institution based in the building, the Wissenschaftlich-Kulturelles Zentrum Bauhaus, thus also addressed questions of architecture, urban and regional development in its seminars and conferences. Ten years later, this institution was renamed Zentrum für Gestaltung, its trusteeship transferred to the GDR's Bauakademie (building academy). Its new director, Rolf Kuhn, arrived from Weimar with a group of planners, architects and urban sociologists and transformed the Bauhaus into a centre for any international debates on urban and environmental development that were possible in the late GDR era. With the concept of the industrial garden realm, these protagonists then developed an idea of how the Bauhaus Dessau could intervene in the social and ecological transformations of the industrial regions of central Germany post-1990. As such, the concept of environment, which was loaded with different connotations, also provided an important topical frame of reference for the institutional history of the Bauhaus Dessau. Thirdly, the Institut de l'Environnement represents a hitherto neglected chapter in the history of radical design pedagogies which put the environment on the agenda in education and research. Given the current pressing need to change ontologies of design, in which design is no longer posited as a unilinear process of shaping a voiceless, infinitely available and passive nature, but rather as reciprocal action in the sense of a coexistence of nature and culture, early attempts to shift the focus from product design to the environment constitute an important intellectual resource—even though the connotations of what was discussed as environment at the time differ radically from what we understand by it now. The shifts in the historiographies towards the ecologies of design and architecture can take into account the multilayered and frequently neglected aspects of the built and designed environment as an ecosystem that is intricately interwoven with its surroundings. These approaches to ecological thinking in the design disciplines likewise inspire the current education, design and research projects of the Bauhaus Dessau Foundation, for they make sense of the role and responsibility of design in an age of planetary crisis. Addressing the legacies of the Institut de l'Environnement and learning about its protagonists have led the international participants of the Bauhaus Lab to consider how such an institute would have to be set up today in order to continue to work on dissolving the boundaries between the humanities, the natural sciences and design disciplines, between teachers and students, between theory and practice, while at the same time decentralising one's own position. The symposium, exhibition and publication of the Bauhaus Lab 2024 will hopefully provide snapshots for a present-day Institut de l'Environnement.

Regina Bittner

‘Where does environ-mental design come in and where does it end? To be honest, no one can really answer that question these days.’

Claude Schnaidt. ‘Ausblick auf das zerklüftete Gelände der Umweltmacher und Umweltbürger’, in: *Umweltmacher und Umweltbürger,* Dresden: Verlag der Kunst, 1982, p. 309. The text is based on a lecture at the University of Geneva in 1972.

FAÇADE MATTERS: JEAN PROUVÉ'S INVISIBLE PRESENCE AND VISIBLE LEGACY IN THE INSTITUT DE L'ENVIRONNEMENT

In December 1969, the Institut de l'Environnement (IE) officially opened on Rue Érasme in the 14th arrondissement of Paris. A mere 21 months later, in September 1971, it was legally dissolved. In the midst of the cultural and educational reforms in late-1960's France, the IE was an experimental project that sought to explore cross-disciplinary pedagogies on behalf of the 'environment.' And while Tony Côme's research through archives and interviews with former trainees, called *stagiaires* at the institute, already shed light on the background of the institution's transfer from Ulm to Paris and its pedagogical activities,[5] the notion of 'environmental pedagogies' still remains fleeting. The aluminium façade panels patented by Jean Prouvé might be the most tangible legacy of the Institut de l'Environnement, and they could provide an alternative vantage point from which to explore its situated history.

The aluminium façade panel became a crucial material starting point for the 2024 Bauhaus Lab's research on the IE. Investigations into Claude Schnaidt's personal archive at the ETH Zurich's gta Archive[6] revealed little direct evidence of Prouvé's involvement in the design process. The decision to use Prouvé's window façade panels appears to have been driven primarily by the practical necessity for the rapid construction of an educational institution. Moreover, this façade panel was not originally developed specifically for this project; it was patented in 1964 and had been used in several public buildings.[7] While archival records do not confirm Prouvé's direct connection with the institute, I argue that his impact on the IE's architecture, pedagogy and legacy merits additional scrutiny.

A panel's history: The Panneaux industrialisés CIMT—Jean Prouvé's façade system and post-war prefabrication movement of school buildings in France

The aluminium panels used on the IE's façade were Panneaux industrialisés CIMT composed of self-supporting sandwich elements arranged on a 180-cm grid. Each element consisted of metal facings and insulating expanded polyurethane, forming a 57-mm-thick structure.[8] These sandwich panels, some with a glass window and some opaque, offered insulation, modular design and factory-based production efficiency. Jean Prouvé's interest in aluminium began in the 1930s and led to the development of numerous products during his collaboration with L'Aluminium Français at the Maxéville factory, a partnership that ultimately ended in failure. In 1954, he returned to Paris and established a new company, Les Constructions Jean Prouvé. His development of aluminium sandwich panel systems began in 1957 when he took over the construction division of the Compagnie industrielle de matériel de transport (CIMT) Lorraine to maintain a tight connection to factory-based production. From then on, Prouvé collaborated with CIMT on the development of mass-produced lightweight prefabrication and curtain wall systems. Though these systems were not created for the Institut de l'Environnement, they were closely tied to broader post-war attempts in France to industrialise school construction.

Since the 1940s, the French Ministry of Education had pursued industrialised school building construction. In 1956, the DESUS, the department for sports and university facilities, established technical and managerial procedures to promote prefabrication nationwide for secondary schools and universities.[9] Prouvé contributed to this movement from 1931 to 1974.[10] Although Prouvé's publicly known uses of CIMT-type panels appeared more in office buildings, such as the CIMT headquarters (architect Emile Deschler, 1963) and the French embassy in Warsaw (architect Bernard Louis Zehrfuss, 1966), the panels were primarily intended for secondary schools. The version applied at the institute was part of a large-scale, lightweight curtain wall system patented in 1965,[11] and it was included in the 'Préfabrication ouverte' programme by 1965, when Jean Prouvé's façade found its place in the top list at national level.[12] The fact that Robert Joly,[13] chief architect of civil buildings and national palaces (BCNP), selected this wall-panel system in 1968 for this reform-oriented educational project thus appears only natural.

Invisible connections: CIMT panels, the Tabouret system and the modularity of the open plan

Prouvé's association with the IE often seems to be limited to the visible CIMT panels, but deeper connections lie in the building's open plan layout. In 1963, he developed the Tabouret system, a prefabricated school system commissioned by educationalists Henri Charnay and Carmona of the Institut pédagogique national (IPN).[14] Based on a simple square module with a grid of 7.20 m, representing a standard classroom, this system employs semifinished products of steel columns and beams assembled dry, using predrilled holes, bolted joints and steel fittings. The aim was twofold: to accommodate new educational spatial requirements emphasising flexibility and to establish a closed prefabrication system allowing Prouvé to 'influence the spatial design of the building without acting as the architect of the projects.'[15] However, due to its rigidity and cost, the Tabouret system was not widely adopted after its invention. Instead, its accompanying CIMT façade wall system was incorporated into the 'Préfabrication ouverte' programme and widely implemented in schools, including the Institut de l'Environnement. Coincidentally, the IE shared the Tabouret system's growing grid system of spatial freedom and used a dry-assembled steel frame structure. Its non-loadbearing partitions, modular grid and dry construction methods closely aligned with the philosophy of the Tabouret system, even if it did not employ Prouvé's column and beam components.

Interestingly, the predecessor of the Institut de l'Environnement—the HfG Ulm—featured a similarly modular façade system, composed of infill grids that could be alternately filled with glazing, solid panels or left open, suggesting a notion of void space. In 1965, Claude Schnaidt hosted a visit by students and faculty from the École des Beaux-Arts to the HfG Ulm, laying the groundwork for its later transplantation to Paris as the Institut de l'Environnement.[16] While the institute is often regarded as an unfinished transposition of the Ulm model into the French context, the use of Jean Prouvé's industrialised façade system suggests that it should also be situated within the broader framework of educational building reforms in France in the 1960s.

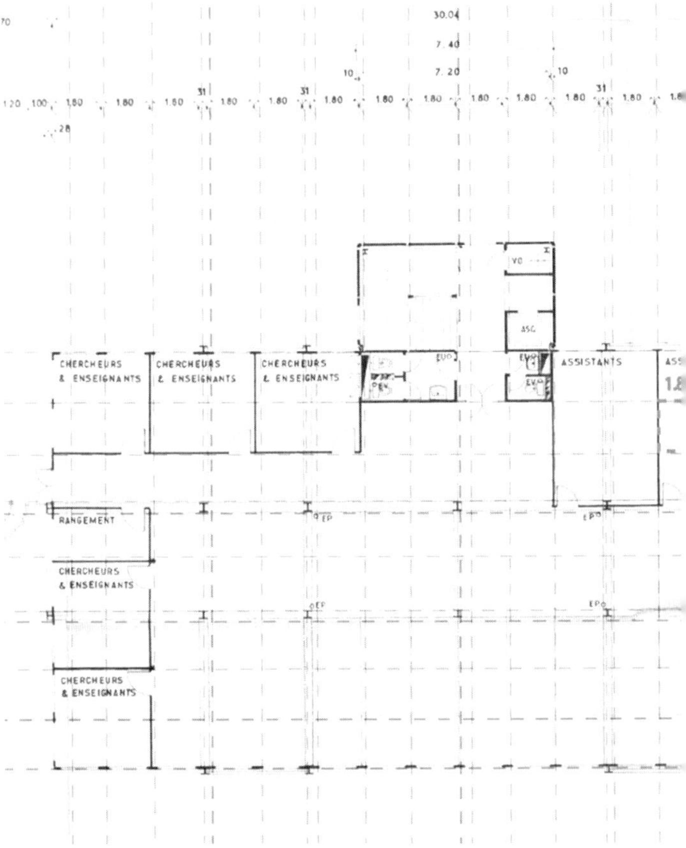
30.04
7.40
7.20
1.80
31
10
28
CHERCHEURS & ENSEIGNANTS
RANGEMENT
ASSISTANTS
ASC
VO
EP

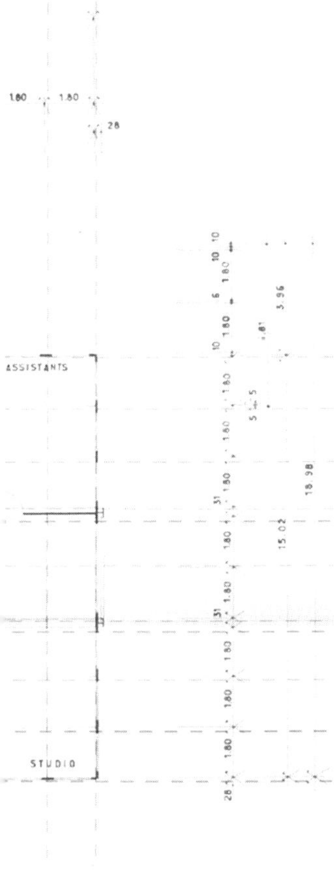

● Fifth floor plan drawing of the Institut de l'Evironnement, Paris, 1969.

In this sense, the Institut de l'Environnement was not so much a direct continuation of the Ulm School but rather a manifestation of France's evolving pedagogical ideals, marked by openness, flexibility and industrialised construction, and the HfG Ulm was just the proper model for this.

● Section and east–west elevations of the Institut de l'Environnement, Paris, 1969.

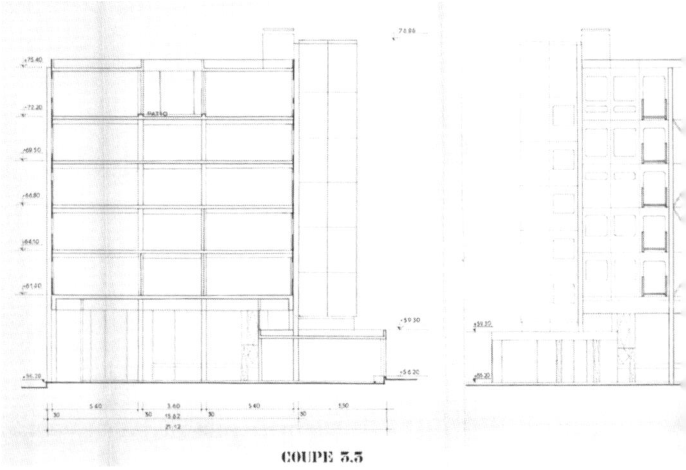

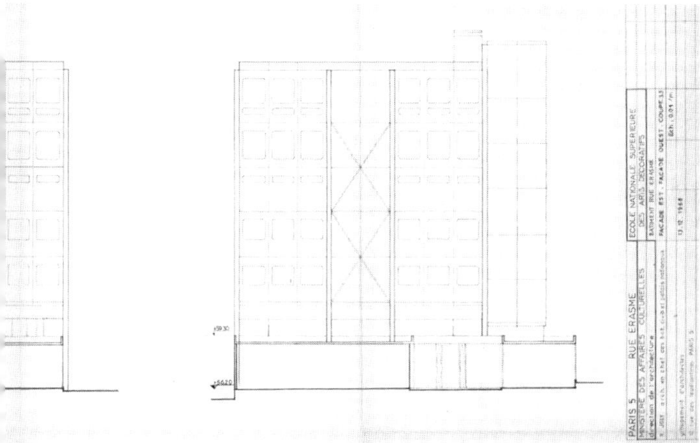

ADE OUEST

FACADE EST

Façade of the Hochschule für Gestaltung Ulm (HfG Ulm).

Façade of the Institut de l'Environnement in Rue d'Ulm, Paris, c. 1971.

Surface and substance: The visible legacy of 'environment' pedagogies

Prouvé's closed system of prefabrication may not have succeeded, but his aspiration to influence school design without direct architectural authorship found partial realisation in the IE. While spatial connections through the Tabouret system may be abstract, the CIMT façade, as a representative image, stands as Prouvé's visible legacy of the institute. In both institutional recollections and promotional materials after its opening, it often reappears as a background motif, symbolising pedagogies of environment. As Akiko Takehara recalls, the IE was a place of lively debates but left little tangible output during the time she was a researcher there. Despite that, she, a non-architect, strongly remembered the IE's façade by Prouvé.[17]

This aluminium 'box' was both architecturally harmonious and symbolically open to pedagogical possibilities. Both journal articles written by Claude Schnaidt to introduce this institute and the in-house publication *Environnement*[18] featured the façade prominently. When demolition loomed in 1993, the Prouvé panels became an argument in favour of the building's preservation, despite his limited direct involvement.

As Schnaidt wrote in 1995 about his collaborator Claude Cobbi, 'That little box was ours, our home of friendship, our unhealed wound, our cradle and our coffin.'[19] The CIMT façade embodied emotional as well as architectural histories, binding together the unrested concerns of environment, pedagogy and reform.

Claude Schnaidt Editorial

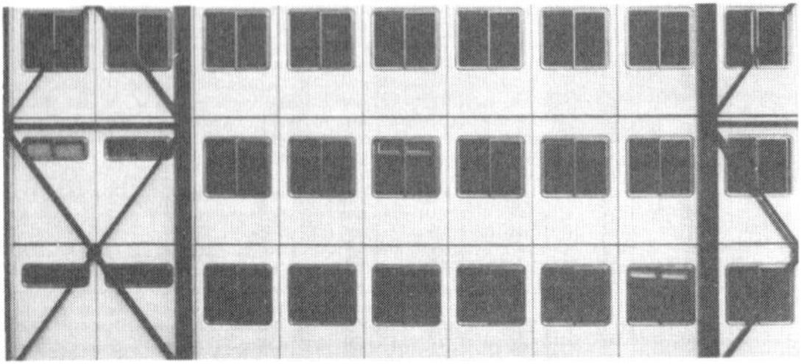

Cette nouvelle revue, dont voici le premier numéro, est l'organe de l'Institut de l'Environnement qui a été créé en 1969 à l'initiative du Ministère des Affaires Culturelles. Parce qu'il est nouveau, parce que toute son énergie a été absorbée jusque là par des tâches d'organisation intérieure et parce qu'il prétend s'occuper d'environnement, on ne sait généralement pas très bien ce qu'est cet institut et ce qu'il veut.

L'Institut de l'Environnement s'attache à promouvoir un renouvellement des enseignements de l'urbanisme, de l'architecture, de l'industrial design et de la communication en formant des enseignants et en conduisant des recherches sur tous les problèmes relatifs à ces enseignements. Pour atteindre ses objectifs, il a organisé :
un cycle de préparation à la recherche et à l'enseignement dans les disciplines concernées par l'aménagement de l'environnement ;
des séminaires s'adressant à des enseignants et spécialistes détachés par leurs établissements ;
des recherches relatives à l'environnement et à son aménagement, ainsi qu'aux enseignements qui s'y rapportent ;
des services, laboratoires et ateliers qui sont à la disposition des différents secteurs de l'Institut et de certains organismes extérieurs.

Lorsque l'idée de l'Institut prit corps, tout le monde ne parlait pas encore en France de l'environnement. La création de notre maison a coïncidé avec la découverte de l'environnement par les politiciens, la grande presse et l'homme de la rue. Or ce déferlement de discours sur l'environnement n'a pas, jusqu'ici, contribué à définir le concept. Bien au contraire. Pour les uns, l'environnement est l'ensemble des choses, des êtres et phénomènes qui conditionne la vie des hommes. Pour d'autres, c'est le milieu naturel et le cadre artificiel inséré par l'homme dans ce milieu. Certains pensent que l'environnement n'est qu'un pseudo-concept. D'autres se l'expliquent par les pollutions, les nuisances et l'exploitation des ressources naturelles. Il y a ceux qui voient dans l'environnement la problématique qui permettra de réconcilier les hommes au-delà des doctrines

1

● Editorial by Claude Schnaidt, page from the first edition of the IE's journal *Environnement*, February 1971.

Epilogue: Through the façade toward the Institut de l'Environnement

The façade remains a contested topic in architectural historiography. With modern technology, it evolved from a structural thick wall to a free membrane separating interior from exterior; meanwhile architects get more freedom when shaping a façade because of this. Yet, the 1968 design of the IE's façade offers an unusual solution: architect Robert Joly relinquished control of the façade to adopt Prouvé's CMIT panels originally designed for the façade of the Tabouret system which in part facilitated the open-plan of the institute.

Pedagogically, the Institut de l'Environnement is often seen as a transplanted fragment of the HfG Ulm, but Prouvé's CIMT façade reveals it as a special case within the context of post-war French school building construction. Prouvé's ideal of closed-systems for school buildings, though unsuccessful in the long term, found unexpected expression in a project emphasising an open, interdisciplinary space for environment pedagogies. The façade thus becomes both the most literal and symbolic surface through which the IE's entanglement with French educational reforms and the prefabrication movement for school buildings is reimagined.

Jie Shen

ON HISTORIOGRAPHIC CONCERNS: CHOOSING AN EVENT, TRACING INTENTIONS AND DIGGING INTO PERSONAL PAPERS

A panel leaning against the wall remains as a trace of what was once a school, evoking the materiality of a building that no longer stands. What is this object? Why was it designed? With what intention? By whom? These might be the first questions posed by a design historian interested in uncovering the trajectory of this artifact. One could start by describing its materiality: a combination of galvanised steel, aluminium and glass. Or inquiring about the fabrication process behind it: the factory responsible for its assembly, the technologies involved in it. Or even its purpose: was it an affordable choice for fast construction or an ideologically modern stance?

Faced with this vestige of the past, we are led to reconstruct meanings, and the possibilities are vast. For historians, this is an assignment that requires archival investigation—a complex process demanding time and concentration, along with feelings of solitude and doubt but also rewards. Slowly, the pieces of a larger puzzle hopefully start coming together through archival practice to form a clearer image of what was initially unclear. However, 'A passion for the archives is not an exemption from its pitfalls',[20] an assertion that became evident to us, the participants of the 2024 Bauhaus Lab edition.

We were a heterogeneous group; some participants had already conducted archival research in their professional practices while others had not. This apparently disjointing aspect actually turned out to be an enriching experience as the relevance of archives emerged as a major point of contention. The group soon realised that dealing with documents from the past requires choices grounded in a fundamental contradiction: while light is shed on what was selected, other materials remain in the shadows of archive drawers—and, consequently, do not become part of historiographical narratives.

Thus, this essay aims to foreground issues that arose during the Bauhaus Lab investigations through my perspective as a design historian on our collective debates. It is a retrospective effort to better comprehend some of the blind spots left by our research on the Institut de l'Environnement (IE) in Paris. It does so by focusing on three main ideas regarding archive matters but also beyond that: choosing an event, tracing intentions and digging into personal papers.

The first of these reflections focuses on the act of choosing a research topic, which is not a self-evident process. Analysed through a historical lens, this choice can reveal crucial aspects of a conducted investigation, helping to clarify the point of view from which a theme is approached. Therefore, choosing an event as relevant is a delicate process—although this aspect is often left unexamined. From the perspective of the French historian Arlette Farge, an *event* is initially a *moment,* which over time and through multiple heterogeneous perspectives—including those of historians—takes form and becomes history. In other words, it is both 'maker and made':[21] while it drives a historiographical narrative, it is also shaped by it. It is, ultimately, not an objective fact in itself.

This process can be better explained considering a shared initial perception we had on the IE, more specifically, on the pedagogical perspective put into practice by the institute. From a contemporary orientation, the word *environment* carries multiple layers of meaning within the field of ecology, which become even more complex when considering its different translations. In a first interpretation, then, part of the group expected the IE would be related to ecological issues in the past, an assertion refuted by the bibliography research we conducted before visiting archives.

In this sense, an initial discomfort that emerged within the group during the early debates can be summed up in the following question: why should we study this particular institute? This concern was especially intriguing to me, since—as Marc Bloch said[22]—the past is seen through the eyes of the present and vice-versa. Reformulating this unease in historiographical terms, I would say we found ourselves at a crossroad. Why isolate this event—the two-year existence of a school in Paris—if perhaps other past episodes would fit the questions we are dealing with in our present better? In parallel to IE's foundation, the intersectionality of design and other issues such as race and class was already brewing up as evidenced by the debates at the International Design Conference in Aspen (IDCA) in 1970.[23] However, it was not a particular issue dealt with by the IE's community.

The fact is that the choice of an event—and its relevance for design education—had already been made by the Bauhaus Dessau Foundation within the framework of its own research interests: investigating exchanges and connections between modern experiences of design education inside and outside Germany. In this regard, the Institut de l'Environnement appears to be a pertinent case, considering that its existence is relatively unknown[24] and that its foundation was mainly instigated by Claude Schnaidt—a Swiss architect who later dedicated himself to the resurrection of the Bauhaus legacy within the GDR during the 1970s. Moreover, he started a relationship between Germany and France, evident in his pedagogical transition from the Hochschule für Design Ulm (HfG Ulm) to the IE. These interests had apparently also influenced the Bauhaus's choice of the archives we would investigate while researching the institute: the HfG-Archiv Ulm in Germany and the gta Archive at ETH Zurich in Switzerland.

The archives keep documents referring to Schnaidt's activities and networks with different focus areas. At the HfG Ulm, he was a student, professor, head of the building department and co-rector, and the HfG-Archiv Ulm preserves documents regarding his life at the school. On the other hand, the gta Archive inherited his private archive and library after his death in 2007. Since Schnaidt was identified as a key figure for the research, it now seems appropriate to address the second point I propose in my reflection: tracing intentions—as we primarily had access to documents from Claude Schnaidt's collection on the IE. For this, I chose a New Year's card that popped up among letters, photographs, tables, texts and graphs kept by the HfG-Archiv Ulm.

• Drawing by Claude Schnaidt for a New Year's card, 1958.

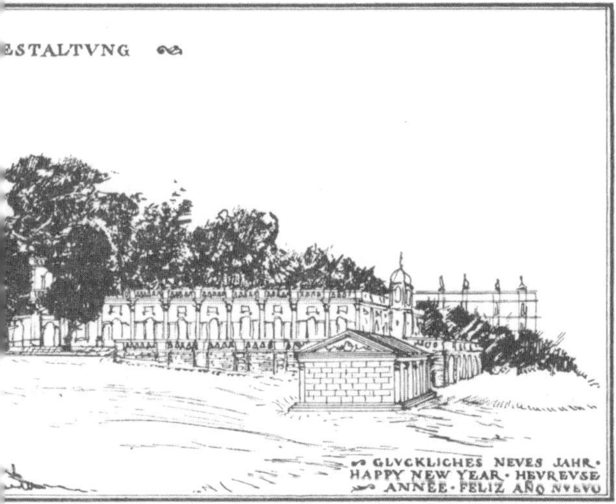

The black-and-white drawing captured my attention due to its incongruity with the Ulm atmosphere; the apparent Versailles Castle is rooted in the iconic topography of the HfG Ulm. Framed by lines, the card wishes the possible receiver a Happy New Year, written by hand in a humanist typographic style. The message 'Happy New Year' appears in four different languages: German, French, English and Spanish. The full name of the HfG Ulm has a central position at the top of this intriguing piece of paper, followed by the year—1958—written in Roman numerals. The unlikely replacement of Max Bill's modernist straight-lined masterpiece with the ornate and theatrical Baroque style reveals the satirical humour of the card's creator.

Behind this audacious joke is Claude Schnaidt. Although still a student at the time of the New Year's card's creation, Schnaidt already demonstrated a critical mindset, a feature that attracted the attention of those around him. Max Bill, then director and teacher at the HfG Ulm, wrote to Schnaidt in February 1956 to warn him about his disruptive behaviour in the building department.[25] Schnaidt apparently promoted opinions on architecture that did not align with Bill's own. Not even the threat of expulsion at the time could deter Schnaidt from maintaining his critical sense of humour, which was still evident two years later in his choice to represent the school as a Baroque castle on a New Year's card—an architectural style, much like the typographic style used for his congratulatory message, rejected by the modernist approach developing at the HfG Ulm.

These documents are important clues to better comprehend Schnaidt's strong opinions also perceivable in two texts he wrote later for *ulm* magazine: 'Prefabricated hope'[26] and 'Architecture and political commitment.'[27] Instigated by Marxist theory, he wrote an elaborate critique of what he described as the lack of commitment and political action among his modernist peers, reinforcing the necessity to stress the relationship of design, science and social engagement—something he believed was not fully achieved in Ulm.[28] From a radical reinterpretation, Schnaidt developed the theoretical basis for creating the IE in 1969, deeply informed by his personality and strong critical stance regarding modernism.

This set of characteristics in Schnaidt leads me to my final consideration: digging into personal papers. Considering his personality and assuming that the processes of self-archiving are not neutral actions but rather opportunities for those who archive to 'make themselves seen as they see themselves and as they would wish to be seen.'[29] It is important to highlight once again the fact that most of the IE documents we found were part of Schnaidt's personal archive, kept by the gta Archive. Indeed, we were mainly dealing with the materials produced within the IE, but ones that have passed through the filter of an individual committed to specific ideologies regarding design, modernism and environment. Beyond that, there was a person ultimately disappointed by the end of a major personal investment less than two years after it was founded.[30]

Which documents did Schnaidt want people to see in the future? What did he decide to keep or destroy? These reflections still intrigue me, and more time than we had would be necessary to trace the nuances of selection, omission, destruction and disappearance that resulted in the small—yet quite significant—portion of documents we were able to access.

Nevertheless, in the exhibition we conceived, we found a way to express what still takes shape in spite of many uncertainties: the archive curtain, composed of a set of interrelated propositions drawn from our archival findings. It resulted from the dialogue between those of us unaccustomed to working with archives—who felt overwhelmed by the amount of information and the difficulty of choosing what to exhibit—and those familiar with this feeling, who saw in it an opportunity to exercise the idea that, in historiography, it may not be the object that matters but rather the meanings developed around it. One vital question remains, though: what are the histories yet to be written through the findings of other archives and testimonies related to the Institut de l'Environnement?

Rafael Amato

Exhibition

On Behalf of the Environment. Pedagogies of Unrest
Presented at the Bauhaus Dessau
Bauhaus Lab 2024

NETWORKS

TROP TARD CRS
LE MOUVEMENT POPULAIRE
N'A PAS DE TEMPLE

STUDIO

"It is about the usage of the student notice board. I believe this involves a matter of principles. In France, students are not allowed to display political views on campus"
"The sds hochschulgruppe ulm is of the opinion that the student body, especially those of a socially committed school, must take a position on political events. The head of such a school should not hinder the political activity of the student body, but rather guarantee its development."
worte für's bauhaus sind gut taten für die hfg sind besser
worte für's bauhaus sind gut taten für die hfg sind besser

TROP TARD CRS
LE MOUVEMENT POPULAIRE
N'A PAS DE TEMPLE

BAUHAUS
HOLA
ME LLAMO

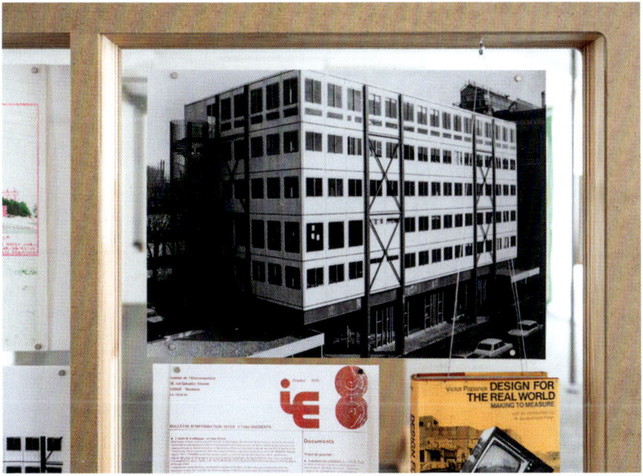
Victor Papanek
DESIGN FOR
THE REAL WORLD
MAKING TO MEASURE
Documents

Institut d

Environnement

CHANGING REPRESENTATIONS: WHAT DOES AN ARCHITECTURAL SYMBOL OF THE ENVIRONMENT LOOK LIKE?

At the beginning of the Bauhaus Lab research, I imagined myself wandering around the streets of Paris's Latin Quarter, just a year after the upheavals of May 1968. There, at the intersection of Rue Érasme and Rue d'Ulm, an industrial-looking building emerges amid the ornate baroque façades of the old university quarter as though it had arrived from another era. This spark of modernity was shaped as a simple rectangular volume clad in aluminium panels, its façade rhythmically punctuated by rounded rectangular windows that circled the building. This unusual building was the home of the Institut de l'Environnement (IE), an innovative institution dedicated to advanced studies of the environment. It was like an island that appeared in the Parisian landscape in the aftermath of May 68, offering a new direction at a time when most of France's art education institutions were in disarray.

The environmental movement—and with it, the discourse on environmental architecture—began to gain momentum in the early 1960s. At the same time, the study of semiotics was rapidly expanding beyond the field of linguistics into the humanities, the arts and social theory. By framing culture as a communicative system based on the exchange of signs and meanings, semiotics provided a powerful basis for rethinking architecture and the built environment as forms of communication. Nevertheless, the semiotics of architecture is challenging for it brings functions and meanings together, side by side.[31] Tomás Maldonado critically argued that architectural semiotics

● Institut de l'Environnement, photo: Alain Leloup, 1970.

relies predominantly on the visual realm. He held the influential thesis *Learning from Las Vegas* by Robert Venturi, Denise Scott Brown and Steven Izenour[32] to be a declaration of blind trust in the visual flat image of reduced architecture. This point of view, he warned, introduces the term 'environment' into a visually originated system of signs, amounting to what he called semiological abuse.[33]

From this perspective it is evident that an institution like the IE must also approach the environment as a cultural and symbolic construct shaped by language and perception. The structure of the Institut de l'Environnement, designed by Robert Joly—chief architecte des bâtiments civils et palais nationaux, an architect specialised in building and site conservation—embodied a quintessential modernist typology: the free plan. A load-bearing structure that frees up large plateaus on every story where people could converge, meet and exchange ideas. As Robert Spizzichino recalled, 'The building had been designed in the spirit of educational renewal and in the spirit of 68. In a nutshell, you had two large trays that were entirely modular ... The teacher-researchers each had a tiny monk's cell. It was therefore impossible for them to hold meetings on their own. Similarly, there was no head and no large main office. Only the administration had proper offices.' [34] This architecture quite literally translated a decompartmentalised pedagogy into an open, modular structure shaped by the modernist typologies of the era. Joly was honoured to invite Jean Prouvé to design the school's façade, incorporating his latest CIMT aluminium panels to clad the building. These prefabricated industrial elements were selected not only due to the tight construction schedule but also to project an image of collective, non-corporatist and grounded architecture. While advocating an industrialised form of construction, Prouvé's vision was rooted in values of social responsibility, practicality and accessibility. His approach to design—whether in structures or furniture—sought to be affordable and human-centred. These principles resonated with the founding ethos of the Rue Érasme institution, aligned with its humanities and social sciences agenda.

Alain Leloup's 1970 photograph—probably the best-known image of the building—shows the institute from a high angle on the west side, likely taken from across the street. The photos offer a clear, three-dimensional view of the box-like structure. Rendered in black and white, the photographs accentuate the cold materiality of the aluminium panels and the strict repetition of clean right angles, evoking a strong visual association with the industrial architecture of a factory.

Can this building be read as a symbol of environmental architecture? At first, it seems to stand out from the Parisian architectural landscape; yet, it does not function as a direct symbol, certainly not in the conventional sense. The building scale remains modest, blending quietly into its surroundings; its height does not disrupt the city's skyline, and its rectangular form is almost anonymous. Although its design language diverges from traditional Parisian motifs, it abstains from overt gestures of symbolism. Rather than a symbol, the building stands as a rigorous embodiment of the ideas that

● Inside an office of the Institut de l’Environnement, photo: Alain Leloup, 1970.

preoccupied architect-theorists in the early 1960s, among them the embrace of the grid, the pursuit of flexibility and a commitment to the notion of a light and affordable construction. It materialises a conceptual architecture, where ideology is not proclaimed but embedded in structure.

The opening photograph of the exhibition, also taken by Leloup, captures an ordinary moment of office life at the institute. Yet, through the frame of the window in the Institut de l'Environnement's façade, the silhouette of the Paris Pantheon appears clearly in the background. This subtle composition reveals an underlying tension in architectural symbolism, drawing attention to what dominates the city's cultural imagery—and from where such iconicity is observed and experienced.

Can architecture represent the environment, and which symbolic language can it embody? As a complex and many-layered term, 'environment' resists any singular or fixed representation—its meanings are multiple, shifting across cultures, between contexts and disciplines. At the IE, the term remained open, serving as a starting point for ongoing inquiry. Claude Schnaidt established this openness, framing the environment as a subject of continuous research, declaring that the study would examine the appropriation process between humans and their living environment. Thus, the environment discussed at the IE is the human environment.[35] In the second issue of the school's magazine, Robert Spizzichino noted that the term was increasingly being used in systems analysis terminology, reflecting a rational and computational intellectual trend.[36] The archival records and the interviews conducted with former *stagiaires* show the institute as a site of varied, often conflicting views where debates over the meaning of 'environment' persisted throughout its short life.

Today, the term 'environment' carries a different meaning. In current discourse, it is largely associated with the natural environment. Meanwhile, the once-broad concept of environmental architecture has splintered into various fields, including sustainable architecture, ecological design, landscape planning, green buildings and others. While these approaches encompass diverse practices, the noted green building concept often narrows the focus to the important, yet limited, aim of enhancing energy efficiency. Nevertheless, this new alluring term goes much further as a representation of environmental architecture, bringing it closer to the use of visual language introduced in *Learning from Las Vegas.*

A green building will often be envisioned as a vertical glass façade inlaid with vegetation that extends to the top. The contested building, 'The vertical forest' by Stefano Boeri in Milan, is a representative example of this genre. The high-rise, wrapped in glass and greenery, powerfully illustrates a new symbolic language of environmental architecture. Vegetation reaching the skyline—perhaps nature itself entering the city's silhouette? One can only speculate what Maldonado would say regarding the merger of the skyscraper's capitalist symbolism with vertical vegetation which symbolises the natural environment. When the environment is reduced to a mere façade motif, it evolves into a mode of 'communicative environmental consumerism.' The result is communication stripped of depth and complexity—what Maldonado might call fictitious communication, a simulacrum of meaning.[37]

Despite the broad meaning of the term, the architectural discourse has often flattened the environment to a visual concept, thereby detaching 'environmental architecture' from the social and political forces that define the spaces where human life unfolds. Ultimately, the meaning of 'environment' is constructed and naturalised by the human subject.

The cultural and human complexity embedded in the environment came to life and turned evident in the central installation of the Bauhaus exhibition: a paper curtain stretching across the space, displaying archival documents from the Institut de l'Environnement. These were thematically arranged to reflect the school's evolving pedagogies and conceptual interpretations. The backside—arguably more evocative than the front—invited visitors to contribute their own visual responses to the term, opening the discourse to subjective and collective reflection. Quickly, the curtain became covered in colourful drawings that exhibited how visitors relate to, think and feel about the environment from within the exhibition site.

What emerged was a vibrant mosaic of interpretations, revealing the inconsistencies between what is personal and what is public, what is neutral and what is man-made; it shows each of the visitors' tangible and intangible surroundings. The installation underscored the impossibility of distilling

● Archive curtain installation.

the environment into a single image or meaning—it exists instead in the overlapping layers of how people live in the world around them, how they perceive and imagine it. This multiplicity reminds us that a singular symbolic form cannot reflect such complexity. While the building of the Institut de l'Environnement was never conceived as a symbol, it embodied a conscious architectural response to one of the term's ideas. In light of this, we are left to wonder which spatial languages and forms might emerge to embody the plurality of meanings tied to the notion of environment.

Or Haklai

‘Our idea was that, in the end, every research topic of the *stagiaires* had to be attuned to all of the disciplines and should relate the disciplines to one another.’

Robert Spizzichino in conversation with Bauhaus Lab members, 2024

INTERVIEW WITH ROBERT SPIZZICHINO (B. 1939), FORMER TEACHER-RESEARCHER

23 July 2024, Paris | abridged transcript

● Robert Spizzichino.

[Bauhaus Lab]
How was the institute born?

[Spizzichino]
It was born from a misunderstanding, a big misunderstanding. André Malraux was the Minister of Culture. He was very attuned to questions of what he called the 'sensitive environment.' For André Malraux, the 'sensitive environment' was a concept tied to culture in general. It was the way that we would receive cultural objects, demonstrations, and the way all of this was developed in the arts. It was the deep relationship between art, maybe nature and man. That was the 'sensitive environment' for him. Malraux said, 'Think work and create this institute for me very quickly.' Especially since all the architecture schools were basically in revolt after May 68. He said, 'I want it to go very fast.'
He assigned Florence Contenay and an administrator, a sort of manager if you will, called Claude Cobbi. He had a very positive and important part. Claude Cobbi was interested in the depth, in the content and not only in the management. First of all, the members [of the committee] asked themselves how to approach this, and they became especially attuned to transdisciplinarity. They were more attuned to questions of 'environment' in the broader sense than Malraux. They were the ones who contacted the Ulm school and contacted Claude Schnaidt and [Manfred] Eisenbeis, who also played a very important role as a founding member.
And this is a misunderstanding, very soon after Claude arrived, it moved towards a much broader sense of transdisciplinarity than the one Malraux was thinking of. The question was no

longer about culture and the 'sensitive environment.' It was 'environmental design'. We went from the concept of 'sensitive environment' to the concept of 'environmental design.'
There was collective research going on. Don't forget that there was a psychoanalyst on the team. And there was an ecologist, not environmentalist, Christian Garnier, who later became president of the Fédération France-nature-environnement. About the topics to be developed, they were told, 'Figure out how to create groups, but stick to the concept of transversality.' You define your topics and your research questions. Quite extraordinary!

[Bauhaus Lab]
How do you remember the *stagiaires*?

[Robert Spizzichino]
There was a big space, and in this space, there were small groups of *stagiaires* in every corner. Sometimes they went from one to the other because they did not like their group, and they would change etc. They produced very very diverse things. You have to understand, they were still marked by May 68. So some of them were focused on contestation before everything, saying, 'We start from scratch and rebuild the world through the 'habitat', urbanism, etc.' There were very interesting ways of doing that.
And then of course Claude's role, who was always an ayatollah of modernism. There were terrible debates. Because people from outside the institute came to talk about things, and every time Claude disagreed, he wrote a note to say why he disagreed, how bad it was, etc. He was an ayatollah, not only of

modernity, but of modernity viewed by a pure Leninist-Marxist. We had very harsh debates inside the institute about concepts, including the definition of transversality, including the role of architecture and urbanism in the modern world.
Anyway, there was a continuous series of debates and sometimes general assemblies of the *stagiaries,* who of course were always rebelling against authority.
Despite all the difficulties we had and despite the very tough debates, afterwards I only met people who remembered it as being wonderful, saying things like, 'Oh, the times we lived in, we lived it!'
This was really characteristic of the institute: the contrast between the harshness of the debates, the concepts, the oppositions … and then what the people got out of it in the end. Whether it's us teachers or the *stagiaires*, it was a very strong characteristic.

[Bauhaus Lab]
What role did systems theory play in your teaching?

[Robert Spizzichino]
We did not teach systems theory so much in a conceptual way. But we were, and this was often my role, trying to extend narrow subjects into transversality. Our idea was that, in the end, every research topic of the *stagiaires* had to be attuned to all of the disciplines and should relate the disciplines to one another.
We pushed for transdisciplinarity, meaning that eventually, elements between the disciplines could possibly create new disciplines. Here is a good example: 'The city as a communication system.' It was done by Manfred Eisenbeis, and I

served as a consultant. For 'The city as a communication system', we introduced a number of disciplines in urban matters, sociology and so on. I intervened on the topic of methodology. I simply took the interactions between technical fields, between theory and practice, between intention and reality, etc. as elements. It was not systems theory as such, but it highlighted interactions in the process.
Nowadays, regarding all the mistakes we have made in the past, all these questions can only be treated in a systemic way. You cannot say that you treat just one problem.

When you treat questions of culture, you are dealing with questions of water, questions of soil, questions of food, questions of the relation between food and habitat, etc. at the same time. You are forced to do this.

[Bauhaus Lab]
Did you also do research on the topic of the environment?

[Robert Spizzichino]
There were no debates about the environment in the current meaning of the term.
Claude was very responsible for it. For him it was all about 'environmental design', and he was not so interested in everything that was too linked to pollution … Back then, we talked about atmospheric pollution, energy difficulties …
and there were also questions of water. This was mostly brought up by Christian Garnier, the ecologist. The courses of Christian Garnier were not attended so much. We did not have any *stagiaires* that were ecologists. We didn't have any.

And the ecological conscience was very undeveloped. The classes by Christian Garnier on the environmental question, although they were remarkable and environmental design was pushed at the times, were not attended much.
Claude had the tendency to underestimate these issues. He was very concerned with the questions of habitat, the lived city ... He believed that behind the notion of environmental design, there was so much to do that everything else was distracting him.

[Bauhaus Lab]
Did you have many international students?

[Robert Spizzichino]
The international side of things was very weak for us. Even though we had diversity, we had *stagiaires* coming from every country in the world. Claude was very sensitive to Germany, to Switzerland, to Europe and the essence of Europe. He was always very interested in the questions of the relationship with the industry, the classic questions of the Bauhaus.
Today we would say that Claude was a productivist. For example, at the conference of the fourth Bauhaus colloquium, he looked at questions of rehabilitation and restoration but you find nothing about the environment, nothing about questions of development besides Marxist concept. I love Claude, he was an extraordinary man, but sometimes he was a bit too dogmatic. He was very attached to the basic Marxist concepts, while the world was changing.
Marc Nerfin came for a lecture at the Institut de l'Environnement on questions of the countries of the South. It was before

Stockholm [United Nations Conference on the Human Environment in Stockholm, 5–16 June 1972], a bit before, to show the extent to which the problems were of a global scale and that the development trajectories in different countries were imperative to take into account etc.
It did not move the institute on this topic … We did embody the concept of 'environmental design', but we could not translate it into French. There were debates about 'environmental design' and the terminology …

[Bauhaus Lab]
Can you tell us why the institute was dissolved? How did it end?

[Robert Spizzichino]
At a certain point, we were under fire from three sides, I would say. Firstly, the new Minister who said that we were communists, Maoists and that we needed to be stopped.
Secondly, some of the *stagiaires* had personal difficulties. They had real personal difficulties, because it was a time that really shocked people. Sometimes we were doing kind of whatever, and this got out.
Then there were some very violent attacks coming from the architecture schools and from the École des Arts Décoratifs from whom we had taken this piece of land. All of this converged to attack us. And so instead of continuing the project and being ambitious about it, we spent too much time dealing with that mess.

[Bauhaus Lab]
If you look back, what was the strength of the institute?

[Robert Spizzichino]
One key point that we need to credit the institute for was the postgraduate programme. Once you have your degree in this or that, it's not enough to tackle questions of the city, environment. etc.
There is a need to learn how to do research, even if you don't want to be a researcher, to learn more about other disciplines. There was a necessity to find forms for this. We thought about pedagogical forms, and we did not want to limit ourselves.
Often people told us, 'You have 70 *stagiaires,* how do you do it for everyone?' So we did think about how to turn it into a normal trajectory for a postgraduate programme, but also possibly for people who have already started working. How does this fit into the continuing studies? There were pedagogical problems. We shouldn't forget that pedagogy was essential.
However, in my opinion, one of the institute's major weaknesses was its approach to connecting what was happening in the institute with real-world problems.

[Bauhaus Lab]
We have found a diagram with all disciplines at the institute crossing each other, can you tell us about it?

[Robert Spizzichino]
There was a crossing between what we called practical axes like communication, architecture, urbanism or design—the basic professions—and the scientific axes. These were psychology, sociology, economics and methodology.

You can see that architecture was not considered a science, but a practice. Just like urbanism, etc.
This crossing was a way to respond to systems theory and to organise transversality. We did not put the disciplines in the same categories. So there were the practical disciplines and the scientific ones, but nevertheless they needed to meet each other.
So, yes, this was our little diagram.

● Claude Schnaidt at the Institut de l'Environnement.

The Institut de l'Environnement (IE) as an institution was so short-lived that, from today's perspective, it almost appears like an event. It existed from the end of the 1960s to the beginning of the 70s, at a time when common understanding about what the environment was had already been shaken.[38] Marked by unpredictabilities and uncertainties, the establishment of the IE in November 1969 was ultimately an experiment. Claude Schnaidt, head of the research institute, was influenced by other institutions and thinkers that spearheaded the relatively new field of environmental design and therefore could provide guidance in a 'rugged terrain.'[39] Schools like the Hochschule für Gestaltung Ulm (HfG Ulm), followed by the Institut für Umweltplanung (IUP) in Stuttgart and the College of Environmental Design (CED) at UC Berkeley, combined the faculties of architecture, design and city planning with social sciences in varying constellations and shaped this emerging field of research.[40]

The growing uncertainties around environmental design are reflected in the work of Horst Rittel and Tomás Maldonado from the same period. Schnaidt was certainly influenced by their thinking as they all taught at the HfG Ulm before Rittel left for Berkeley in 1963 and Maldonado for Princeton in 1966.

Rittel had been working on a theory of design from the perspective of systems thinking since 1958 while teaching at the HfG Ulm and later at the CED. He defined design as a process of modifying the relationship between the user and their environment—an intervention that inevitably had a political dimension to be critically reflected upon. He also emphasised that the complexity of design problems usually requires the collaboration of multiple disciplines.

Rittel's fundamental assumptions significantly overlap with the early concepts of environmental theory published by the IE. In the second—and also final—issue of *Environnement,* the institute's publishing organ, Robert Spizzichino proposed an initial hypothesis: 'The environment can be considered as a complex system of relationships between processes, themselves more or less complex, for a given space and whatever the scale of this space is (from a region to a housing unit).'[41] From this systems-oriented perspective, the environment emerged as an increasingly difficult concept to define. 'Can we manage or control an environment that is itself so difficult to grasp? By virtue of what requirements, what criteria, what system of political, social and economic values?'[42]

● Horst Rittel at the HfG Ulm.

Not only did the definition of what the environment is become increasingly unstable; the idea of planning as a mechanism of control and improvement was also called into question. In a paper on planning from December 1969, Horst Rittel and his colleague Melvin Webber presented a disturbing conclusion: 'Planning problems are inherently wicked',[43] meaning that planning problems involving multiple public stakeholders with conflicting interests can't truly be solved. Rittel and Webber explained their definition of the 'wicked problem' by observing that a solution depends on a precise definition of the problem—yet this is exactly what such projects fail to provide. So, is environmental planning inevitably left with the task of continuously problematising issues instead of resolving them?

The growing doubts concerning 'research into the environment and its development'[44] are also reflected in the article 'Hypothèses pour une theorie de l'environnement' in *Environment* 2, in which Spizzichino emphasised that the theory developing at the IE is in a state of collective reflection. He describes the IE as an 'open laboratory of ideas'—leaving room for uncertainty.[45] Was the described lab-like 'state of reflection' ultimately a step towards certainty or an achievement in itself?

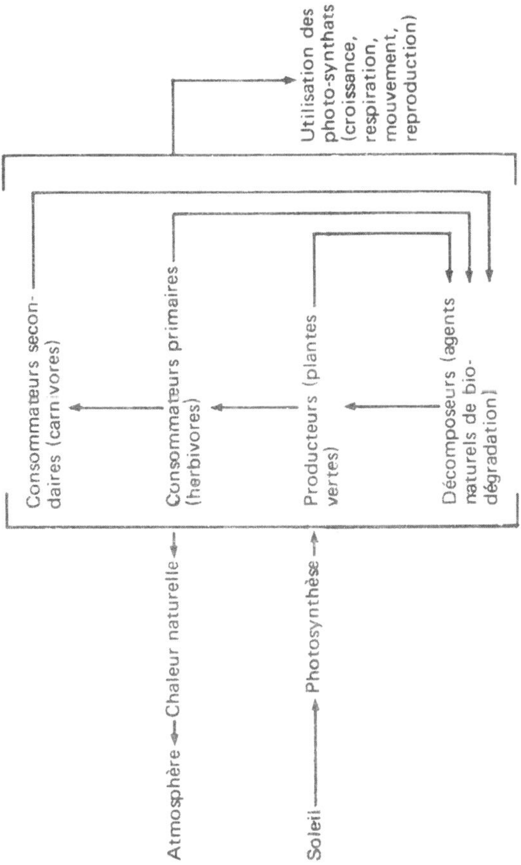

● Diagrams for an environmental theory by Robert Spizzichino.

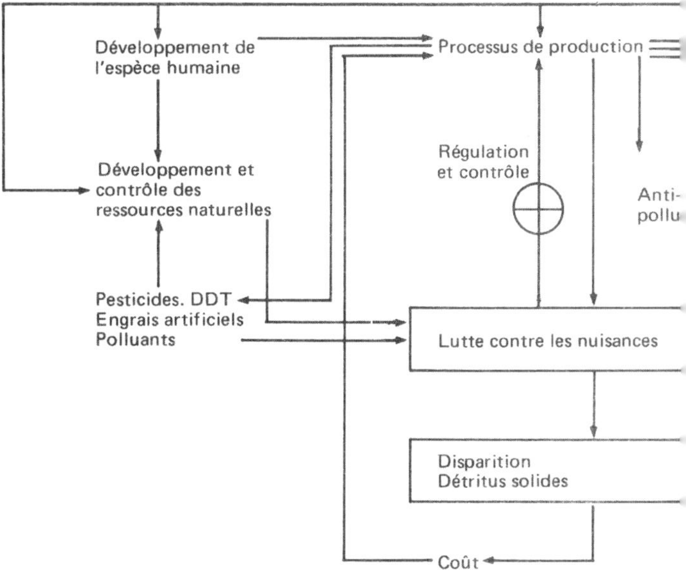

● Diagrams for an environmental theory by Robert Spizzichino.

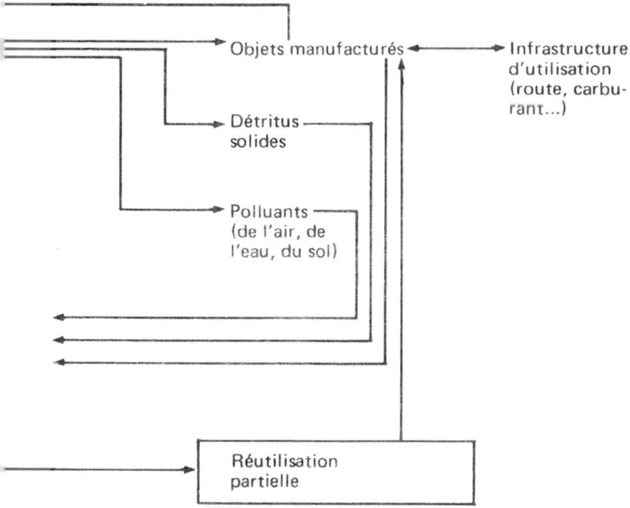
Objets manufacturés
Infrastructure d'utilisation (route, carburant...)
Détritus solides
Polluants (de l'air, de l'eau, du sol)
Réutilisation partielle

However, within this collective openness, Schnaidt anticipated a dangerous trap that had to be avoided. He used the image of cliffs that have to be manoeuvred around and introduced the notion of navigation. The dissolution of disciplinary borders allowed the institute to explore a wide range of interconnections and to address complex questions that could only be solved through a transdisciplinary approach. Nonetheless, this came with challenges: on the one hand, there was the risk of fragmentation. When questions become too broad or unfocused, they can no longer be meaningfully answered—an observation very much in line with Rittel. On the other hand, overly narrow perspectives had to be avoided—for instance, ignoring broader societal or ecological problems in the design process. Therefore, the institute had to navigate between those two cliffs.

Maldonado, too, used the metaphor of a cliff. His essay *Umwelt und Revolte* reflects on state-of-the-art methodologies in environmental design.[46] As explained in the preface to the book, Maldonado turned the initial project into a conceptually open essay. Considering the mismatch between utopian ideals and political realities, he refrained from formulating definitive solutions. In this context, the cliff represents uncertainty about whether the designer can act as an autonomous agent of change. Can he be certain he is not serving the very forces he aims to oppose? That his intentions are not diverted?

Maldonado advocated for a 'constructive scepticism'—seeking to reconcile hopeful visions (utopia) with real-world conditions and scientific methodologies. According to Maldonado, there is no certainty. Despite reasonable doubt,

● Tomás Maldonado teaching at the HfG Ulm.

he pleaded for the designer to act—even more so in the face of pressing ecological problems. His reasoning aligns well with the concept of navigation, which also aptly reflects the modus operandi of the IE.

The practice of navigation implies a constant mode of adjusting and re-positioning. Navigational techniques aim to locate the navigator's position in relation to known patterns, allowing for deviations from established paths. The institute for its part did not only navigate a contested, 'post-Berkeleyan' [47] field of research but also a heavily politicised discourse. Accounts of former *stagiaires* describe lively gatherings and discussions in a politically charged atmosphere—still under the impression of the students' protests in May 1968.[48] Monique Eleb, researcher and psychologist, remembers that the institute 'was an intellectual melting pot, a crucible of exchanges and social and intellectual claims where there was a desire to test new ideas in order to change society. There was a cafeteria and a terrace where people got together every morning to talk. I even met Michel Foucault and Roland Barthes there.' [49] The institute certainly made a strong impression on researchers and students, leaving them with unresolved questions and methodological openness—preparing the ground for future networks of researchers and designers.

Teresa Häußler

● Cover of *L'Architecture d'Aujourd'hui*, no. 145, 'Nouvel environnement.'

HOW TO FIGHT *FORGETTING* IN DESIGN EDUCATION. NOTES ON THE LECTURE *ENVIRONNEMENT ET SOCIÉTÉ* BY TOMÁS MALDONADO (1970)

A radical pedagogy without radical thought and training does not generate the necessary change.[50] This statement becomes especially relevant in the global context of May 1968, marked by fundamental questions about education and society. How do we break down institutional barriers without falling into new limitations? Is it possible to think freely within a system?

The Institut de l'Environnement (IE) was founded to break with established pedagogical canons, betting on multidisciplinary and environmental training. This is reflected in number 145 of the magazine *L'Architecture d'Aujourd'hui.* The edition with the subtitle 'Nouvel Environnement' dedicated two pages to its upcoming inauguration: a centre for the renewal of teaching disciplines that contribute to environmental planning.[51]

Environmental design reflection and thought dominated the institute's agenda, and a significant part of its energy was spent trying to understand the ontology of the term. Claude Schnaidt, in the first editorial of the journal *Environnement,* had the opportunity (and felt the need) to clarify the vagueness that had become evident at the time.

'For some, the environment is the set of things, beings and phenomena that condition human life. For others, it is the natural surroundings and the artificial framework inserted by humans into this environment. There are those who see in the environment an issue that will allow people to reconcile beyond doctrines and ideologies. … As for us, we know that we want to respond to the cultural need for integration of knowledge in the process of appropriation between humans and their environment.'[52]

The central debate, both within and outside the institution, focused on understanding and defining the environment as a concept, but also as a methodological approach to the implications of environmental design.

Alongside these theoretical concerns, the IE placed great importance on the idea that good teaching is impossible without a strong foundation of research to support it.

Reflecting this commitment, the lecture series for the 1970/71 period featured Tomás Maldonado, who had previously served as director of the Hochschule für Gestaltung Ulm (HfG Ulm) from 1964 to 1967. The lecture was called *Environnement et Société*, and its title echoed his recently published work *Umwelt und Revolte. Zur Dialektik des Entwerfens im Spätkapitalismus*[53] which over time would become a reference text, contributing early and decisively to the establishment of an international discourse on environmental design.[54]

● Students at the IE auditorium during a conference, gta Archive/ETH Zurich, estate of Claude Schnaidt.

With a single slide, Maldonado structured the lecture around US president Richard Nixon's neo-Malthusian environmental project, the awakening of youth movements and the countercultural ideology of the environmental movement in the United States.[55] He started his lecture in an ironic tone, noting that society had just discovered that the environment exists. In his *pessimismo costruttivo* stance, he graphically described how in technical civilisation, the dog chases its own tail in a desperate attempt to resolve the effects of environmental pollution.

How does circular logic work? Graphically, the author revealed how the productive system creates a vicious cycle of pollution. The productive system, in order to accelerate the life cycles of renewable resources, creates artificial fertilisers and pesticides. In this profit-driven mechanism, the factories that produce fertilisers are the same ones that produce pesticides, creating a vicious cycle of pollution and financial interests.

At what point in history did the *necessity* become a need? Referencing Henri Lefebvre and his theory of needs, Maldonado stated that the great revolution of consciousness which society must necessarily undergo is to question the problem of the proliferation of objects. Nixon's project was based on limiting or controlling the birth rate in the world leading to less demand and consumption of products and consequently, less waste and pollution. However, Maldonado considered the neo-Malthusian belief to be a fallacy and argued that reality shows the developed countries and their fetishism to be the main consumers of the product stock, not the developing countries.

When asked by a listener about the possibilities of intervention by those who work and write for and about environmental disciplines, Maldonado responded that designers have been and continue to be responsible or co-responsible for the situation due to their lack of critical awareness and their focus on providing a service to the client without considering the final use of their contribution. The private automobile, air conditioning in homes, pesticide abuse and nuclear radiation are all characteristic of technical civilisation, an irreversible civilisation that must infuse a new intention of humanism, a new concern for social layers.[50] He emphasised that society has accepted many things for 40 years out of laziness—intellectual laziness, moral laziness. And he affirmed: we have had comfort, and we have been offered better comfort. In recent years, we have been living without any sensitivity to the social cost of things. Without conclusions or formulas with answers, Maldonado, in his best style, opened the state of the issue to collective debate and reflection.

More than half a century after that conference, the relevance of his observations remains remarkable. It is overwhelming to see how the issues he addressed have steadily worsened over time.

What is the social cost of environmental ignorance? The repercussions are multifaceted and far-reaching, encompassing environmental degradation, biodiversity loss, climate injustice and social exclusion. Currently, the construction industry generates 40 per cent CO^2 emissions, and the development of artificial intelligence (AI) is evolving day by day while the gap in terms of social justice, equity and inclusion in cities continues to widen; in this context, design education faces an enormous challenge.

Congresses, exhibitions, biennials[57] and architecture competitions issue international calls to think of ways, find alternatives and seek creative solutions that actively transform the reality in which we live. We are on a planet in transition that demands a change in the control system that regulates needs and the proliferation of objects.[58] The earth does not generate waste or externalities; only humans do. We need to learn to build by internalising environmental externalities and balancing the economies of construction with the ecologies of production.[59]

Recovering these texts and making them speak from today's perspective allows us to keep memory alive and think about alternative, innovative approaches to the current times. Radical pedagogy without radical thought and training does not generate the necessary change, but reflection, visibility and action around these issues can lead to a profound transformation of the way we understand and relate to the environment. Paraphrasing Maldonado's famous article, this essay does not fight *complacency* but forgetfulness.[60] Revisiting history, thinking with others and reflecting upon alternatives for design education in the near future is the most radical approach we can take today. This is what true revolutions consist of nowadays.

María Paszkiewicz

‘It was truly a paradise. Every time I went to the institute there were only debates. There was a big hall, and there were lots of people. Not *students*, they were stagiaires, you know. All the *stagiaires* were in one room. All of them.’

Akiko Takehara in conversation with Bauhaus Lab members, 2024

INTERVIEW WITH AKIKO TAKEHARA (B. 1940), FORMER *STAGIAIRE*

24 July 2024, Paris | abridged transcript

● Akiko Takehara.

[Bauhaus Lab]
Something that is missing in all the texts about the Institut de l'Environnement is the economic situation of the *stagiaires.* Can you tell us about it?

[Takehara]
It was in 1968. They did not have many resources. They did not find work. But at this moment, Mr Cultural Minister Malraux had also thought about the resources of young people. It was an extraordinary idea. You worked part-time in the morning. The courses only started in the afternoon to guarantee that you could earn money.

[Bauhaus Lab]
The scholarship from the institute was only half of the minimum wage. That is one of the aspects that interest us.

[Takehara]
So yes, half of the minimum wage is not enough to sustain yourself in Paris. But the students were much smarter. You cannot imagine how they learnt to make it with what they had. Boys and girls came together to live together. They were friends. By living in pairs, we did not have to work anymore. That's smart! So they could do anything they wanted. That was our paradise.
It was truly a paradise. Every time I went to the institute there were only debates. There was a big hall, and there were lots of people. Not students, they were *stagiaires,* you know. All the *stagiaires* were in one room. All of them. Some were saying, 'I'm a Marxist', 'I'm a Leninist', 'I'm a Maoist.' Oh, how

these three fought! I never heard talking about architecture, design, the projects ... Nothing!

[Bauhaus Lab]
Only politics?

[Takehara]
Only politics. I really liked it.

[Bauhaus Lab]
And about the environment? Were there any debates about it?

[Takehara]
No teaching, there were only debates. That is my memory of it. Maybe others wrote about debates of the environment … but it was very very nice, very nice, because I did not even know the difference between Maoism, Leninism, etc. So suddenly I discovered the whole leftist world of France. The country of 1968. And the students were very friendly. Absolutely friendly.

[Bauhaus Lab]
Did you notice a big difference between France and Japan in the debates?

[Takehara]
Listen, in Japan, all the events ended in 1970. Since then, nothing. Because there was so much damage, so many dead. For the students, the events of 70, all the young people watching this just thought this is useless. So they do not

feel political. Absolutely not. They were not concerned with politics. Even now, there are no protests or anything. This is the huge difference between France and Japan. That's why the term 'environment' is going down. Disappearing even.

[Bauhaus Lab]
And how did you arrive at the Institut de l'Environnement?

[Takehara]
I was a scholarship holder of the French government. It was in 68, long ago! Since 68 was an event, your government did not want me to come to learn a bit of French for two months in Paris. 'You cannot come yet, we tell you when you can leave.' So I waited in Tokyo until I could leave. They said, 'Okay, now you can come, because the students have left.' So I arrived on 1 September and I was immediately interested in the decorative arts. I was signed up at the school of decorative arts (ENSAD).
I chose Mr Roger Tallon, do you know about him? The one who designed the TGV. He was really a funny person—friendly, who had many very human ideas. At the ENSAD I was attending the classes. But one day Roger Tallon calls me like this and says, 'Akiko, you have nothing to do here. ' Because back then I was already a designer at Canon. Tallon was free to create an office for the design programme. So all this time, he was telling me do this, do that. My scholarship was for two years. The third year I was very worried. I still wanted to live in Paris! I asked Tallon, 'Can you do something?' He said, 'I have a good idea. Just next to here … [The old ENSAD building was situated right next to the Institut de l'Environnement.]

So my registration was already transmitted and the money was sorted so that I could enter there.

[Bauhaus Lab]
Were the amounts of the scholarship from the government and the salary you got as a *stagiaire* at the institute similar?

[Takehara]
Much less for the *stagiares.*

[Bauhaus Lab]
Ah, so it was much less.

[Takehara]
It was not a problem because at this time I only ate at the restaurant.

[Bauhaus Lab]
The restaurant?

[Takehara]
The university restaurant. We could eat there. And in the morning I would take a container like this in my pocket. That's how I survived!

[Bauhaus Lab]
And do you have a special memory of your time at the institute, a strong point?

[Takehara]
Two. The first is that Jean Baudrillard came as a guest speaker. He was brilliant back then. Everyone talked about him because he was the one who said first, 'We are only buying signs.' You are not buying anything, only Chanel, because Chanel sells. That was the one who, for us, was very innovative on the theoretical level. The consumer society is made up of signs. So yes, he was very interesting as a guest speaker.
The second revelation was another guest speaker. They had invited Monsieur ... an Italian.

[Bauhaus Lab]
Ettore Sotsass?

[Takehara]
Yes, Sotsass! He was our god. So of course he brought his red typewriter. What was it called? Olivetti. That's it. He put it like this on the table. We thought he was going to talk about that. No. He took a Leica photocamera out of his pocket. This, you already know very well. This you do not know so much about yet, but the essence of this camera is it's heart of design. It's not that you get better pictures from it. But look at this—he did like this [pressing the camera's shutter button].
He took the Leica M2, and he did this. He passed around the camera to everyone—about 20 *stagiaires.* 'Here you can put 30 m. Then you can put 50, it doesn't matter which. Did you feel the "push"?' So it's really something unexpected, but with 30 m, in the beginning it's very soft, then in a moment: 'click'! It means, they are telling you 'now the picture is taken.' So that is design.

[Bauhaus Lab]
That's amazing. Was there a roll of film in the camera? Do you know? Were there pictures taken during this experimentation round?

[Takehara]
No. Unfortunate.

[Bauhaus Lab]
Were there other international students at the institute?

[Takehara]
Yes, definitely! Spaniards, the Italians, even the Germans, Poles. There were many nationalities. Unfortunately there were no Asians.

[Bauhaus Lab]
What was your impression of the collective work with the other *stagiaires* and the professors? Did your Japanese training have an influence on the way you worked there? Were there any cultural differences in your way of working? And how did you experience this at the institute?

[Takehara]
Ah, absolutely. Us Japanese do not discuss so much. Here in France you start by discussing.
That's the difference. So I do something, I put my results on paper, and I show it. That's my way of working. However, here they start discussing what we should or shouldn't do and they end up doing nothing! But still, for me it was a good idea.

It really nourished me. That's why I wanted to stay in Paris. And I did not realise that here in Europe the architect was considered a god. When I said I was a designer, I work for Canon, all the people, the friends, even very intelligent people would say, 'Oh no, you work for the industry.' They looked down on it. One time a Japanese friend, who was an architect, came to visit me for a few days. I was taking a walk with him. And since he was an architect, people were like, 'Oh, an architect!.' The word 'architect' he was already appreciated and admired. That's the difference here.
I also did some research on why they are considered gods. The first answer was that they were the people who built the church, that is so close to god! That's why they are held in such high esteem. That's why they first serve god. So god and then architecture.

[Bauhaus Lab]
But at the institute, did the architects work together with designers and others?

[Takehara]
Absolutely not. They are so high up. Even in Japan. They see themselves as very very high up.

[Bauhaus Lab]
And did interdisciplinarity work at all or not?

[Takehara]
Interdisciplinarity, the different disciplines that come together? I don't think they came together.

[Bauhaus Lab]
Was it always separated?

[Takehara]
Always separate. God stays god, god does not descend to hell. Because one very clear thing, architecture is for a single unique object. Even if they produce small apartments, one-million apartments, that is not their work. That's just on the side. The architect is in Paris for a museum or a monument. That's their work. They only think about this one thing in relation to society and usage.
But we designers think about everyone. Since she is very small and does not have much strength, how can she still use this machine? And how do you, who is big and strong, manipulate this machine in the same way? That's the difference. So we are for the people. They are only for those with money. It's impossible to come together, to work together with them. Even as a friend or ... in the end, we do not understand each other.

[Bauhaus Lab]
Could 'environment' be a concept that unites the architects and the designers?

[Takehara]
What was nice was that all the disciplines cross each other, and we all take positions.
The idea was good. The reality was far from perfect.

[Bauhaus Lab]
What role did the teachers have at the institute?

[Takehara]
At the institute? I don't understand.

[Bauhaus Lab]
The teachers. Which role did they have, and what was your relation to them?

[Takehara]
Friendly. Otherwise, I did not see them as teachers, but I saw them as friends. That's how it was. We were friends.

[Bauhaus Lab]
And they participated in the debates?

[Takehara]
They were not so old. They were quite young. Not a big age difference. Maybe 5 or 10 years, not even. We were really the same.

[Bauhaus Lab]
Were nature and ecology a topic at the Institut de l'Environnement?

[Takehara]
Ecology back then was not the same ecology as we have today. There was something worse that was happening in Japan: pollution! We did not talk about the rising temperature—not yet, it was just the 60s. The ozone problem was barely starting. The word environment was not so present. It started maybe in the 90s.

[Bauhaus Lab]
So, the way ecology was a part of the institute, was only as pollution? Was this the only environmental phenomenon you studied there?

[Takehara]
I never studied it. For me, the word environment is very new. At the institute there was a different notion of environment. That's why it was interesting to me. The notion that all the facets that surround us form the environment.

[Bauaus Lab]
Our last question: what are the lessons we can learn from the Institut de l'Environnement that are still important today?

[Takehara]
That's hard to say. I never thought about this before. Wait one second. Maybe not a lesson, but the building was drawn by Prouvé and was made of aluminium.
Every time I saw this aluminium architecture, I thought to myself, 'The world has changed.'
That's my lesson. My good memory about the architecture and this aluminium material.
Have you never seen the building?

[Bauaus Lab]
Yes, we have seen the pictures.

[Takehara]
No, in real life! How is he called, the architect who destroyed it?

The one who drew the ENSAD? [The architect of the building that replaced the IE.]

[Bauhaus Lab]
Philippe Starck.

[Takehara]
Maybe. I was so angry. At least it should have stayed as a monument. Sad, very sad. So Prouvé stays with me as a good memory.

[Bauhaus Lab]
Maybe a last aspect that would interest me personally a lot is how you experienced the time of the decline and closure of the institute in 1971.

[Takehara]
I immediately went to Japan. It wasn't necessary, because I did not know there were some parts that moved to Nanterre. It was all happening so fast. I thought, I have permission to leave. I thought I would just come back later. But the spaces were closed. It was so sad. Rue d'Ulm, yes. Maybe that was the final point to a part of my youth. There it goes. It was very short actually.
Two years. Yes, but actually it was good to close it after two years.

[Bauhaus Lab]
It was good to close it?

[Takehara]
Because it presses it like a diamond that you cannot break. It stays like a diamond. That's very good.
And the Minister of Culture, he was the one who had the excellent idea. It was him who in this time created the Musée imaginaire as well. I would say, he is the most respectable Minister of Culture of France. André Malraux. It was him who created the institute! Really, a charming man. Absolutely charming.

[Bauhaus Lab]
And did he come to the institute?

[Takehara]
I never saw him at the institute but I heard he was there.

'It was like a diamond that you cannot break.'

That's how Akiko Takehara, a former *stagiaire,* recalls the pedagogical experiment of the Institut de l'Environnement (IE) in Paris. Her reflections are not just nostalgic musings; they are testimonies to a revolutionary time in design and architecture education. In the wake of the 1968 social unrest, pedagogical experiments bloomed across the globe. These short-lived experiences attempted to go against the grain of institutional education and to reframe contemporaneity. As Beatriz Colomina writes about 'radical pedagogies' of that time, 'even after their apparent destruction, their ideas linger and their networks persist.' [61] The Institut de l'Environnement, I would argue, should be assimilated into these radical experiences as an attempt to create a new learning environment, an 'école décloisonnée',[62] an open and decompartmentalised school within the rigid French university system.

If radical pedagogies transformed institutional knowledge in 1968, today, their unorthodox teachings have been engulfed by our contemporary institutions. What can we still learn from these experiences, especially from the point of view of 'educational projects'? [63]

I write this text from the perspective of a designer who has been engaging in the formal education system as a pedagogue, but who has also been exploring the academic margins through the Living Summer School, a seasonal educational platform in Belgium. Studying the IE was a reflexive experience of the kind of education I was shaped by and of the education that I shape for others. This is especially true because our inquiry was guided by the perspective of an 'educational organiser', Claude Schnaidt, the director of the IE, a figure whose positionality is very different from my own and would deserve further scrutiny. The encounter with his perspective through archival research made evident the still ongoing struggle to liberate ourselves from the violence of institutionalised learning environments. It also deepened my understanding of my own entanglement with educational institutions, of being their product and being someone who works within and against their structures. In this text, I reflect upon researching the Institut de l'Environnement, trying to create bridges between then and now, between the institutional and the experimental.

The tension between 'systematic education' and trying to break away from it was an immanent condition for the IE. A detail that exemplifies this ambiguity is a choice of terminology within the school. Learners were not referred to as 'students' but as *stagiaires*. More than a semantic choice, this term connoted learners as apprentices, as professionals, and it denoted a hands-on approach to learning within the institute. Claude Schnaidt, as reported by Robert Spizzichino in one of our interviews, wanted to create a truly 'postgraduate' programme in which professionals from different backgrounds could convene and learn in a reflexive rather than an instructional way.

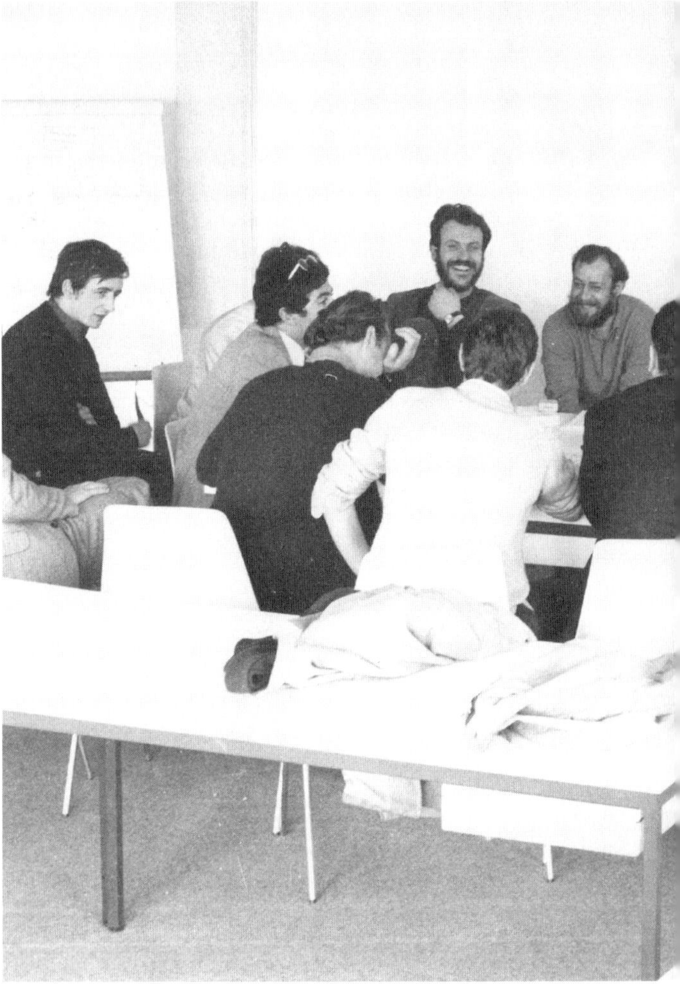

• *Stagiaires* and *enseignants-chercheurs* in discussion.

This marked a drastic departure from the Beaux-Arts model to which architects were subjected before 1968, imitating the work of teachers to reach academic proficiency. Although the term *stagiaire* still implied the presence of a master, it represented a meaningful shift. Even before encountering the history of the Institut de l'Environnement, I have been implementing similar ideas calling every individual who partakes in my educational projects, such as the Living Summer School, 'participant.' This has been a deliberate choice to shift roles starting with language, stressing an active and situated agency in knowledge co-production.

Further underpinning the IE's inclination toward more equitable learning conditions was the stipend of 500 francs per month granted to *stagiaires,* roughly the equivalent of 600 euros today taking into account historical purchasing power. This is a gesture of institutional care that acknowledged the cultural and knowledge labour *stagiaires* contributed to. Remunerating learners is a step towards dismantling institutional hierarchy, at least within the constraints of a capitalist framework. This act raises crucial questions for those of us working on peer-to-peer learning models today: how can we develop remuneration models that align with open, cooperative learning efforts? Which infrastructures and configurations of financial care are truly needed to sustain a pedagogical ecosystem?

Admission procedures at the IE also offer a glimpse of participatory institutional creation. As Tony Côme reports, staff asked prospective *stagiaires* questions such as, 'What would you like to find in the institute?' or 'In your opinion, what should be the place and role of the Institut de l'Environnement in the current school and university context?',[64] thus probing not only applicants' motivations but also aspiration, inviting prospective *stagiaires* themselves to co-construct the programme in a bottom-up manner. Gérard Paris-Clavel noted in our interview that student assemblies were also consulted in the process of establishing the IE. And yet, a persistent tension remained around the *stagiaires'* true empowerment. Archival documents suggest that their influence on the institute's direction was limited and subject to constant negotiation.

How much room was there, really, for critique and transformation from within? This tension, which I also encounter in my work in conversation with fellow educational organisers,[65] can be rephrased as: how can we create intersectional safe spaces or rather brave spaces[66] where learners can intervene and shape education on equal footing with organisers? Foundational conditions such as financial instability, political tensions and individual precarity influence organisational inclusion as much today as they did at the time of the IE. These unresolved questions speak to the fragility of experimental learning environments and the difficulty of sustaining openness within institutional frameworks alike. Much work is still left to do for educational organisers to create sustainable models for inclusion, something the IE, ultimately, did not have the chance to fully articulate before its dissolution.

Another barrier that was questioned within the institute was the separation between pedagogy and research. In fact, the pedagogical staff was composed of *enseignants-chercheurs,* teacher-researchers, who simultaneously investigated environmental design and its pedagogies while attempting to implement these ideas in real time within the IE. Their positioning between theory and practice, research and teaching, the environment and its pedagogical methods is still an interesting framing for formal and informal education. It inspired in me a vision of research not as something to be delivered but something to be lived collectively, messily and in the moment. The open-space design at the IE meant that the staff could work alongside *stagiaires,* dissolving distinctions between instruction and inquiry, authority and dialogue.

Enseignants-chercheurs facilitated different educational actions. Firstly, *stagiaires* followed an elective seminar series in architecture, urban planning, communications and industrial design. Secondly, a big component of the learning experience happened in what might be called 'project-based learning' as *stagiaires* were grouped into multidisciplinary teams that carried out research on negotiated topics with *enseignants-chercheurs.* Initially academic, this research was left open-ended in terms of outputs: architectural models, zines, masks, reports and more were produced. Moreover, learning was enriched by field trips and site visits as well as expert lectures which were normally followed by animated debates. State-of-the-art laboratories complemented the learning environment.

Our archival experience exposed us only marginally to *stagiaires'* works, yet a few key voices emerged that still resonate with pedagogues' concerns today. One of these voices within Claude Schnaidt's archive, Marie Madeleine Michel, proposed the creation of a space within the institute where the body and embodiment could have a legitimate role in pedagogies, learning from underground movements and counterculture.[67] Despite the nonconformist, almost hippie inspiration, this reads today as a call for a liberationist pedagogy. It can act as a reminder for us pedagogues that education is somatic, shaped by rhythms of rest, nourishment and care. Designing educational experiences entails shaping these rhythms and, critically, tending to the bodies that occupy pedagogical spaces. In 1973, this was a radical proposition. It still is.

In another rare testimony of students' voices, Dominique Spinetta writes in his research on critical teaching, 'May 68 accelerated the prism of political awareness among students and teachers and allowed the idea to take hold that architecture is political, that politics is present at all levels of the act of building, that space is not neutral.'[68] Spinetta went as far as prompting demands for the integration of Marxist economics into the architectural curriculum. His opinion stands in contrast to a long-standing tradition in postmodern design, one that continues to this day, which frames design primarily around 'ethics and values'[69] while relegating politics to a 'constitutive outside' of the profession. Spinetta's research remains relevant, especially in the context of (contemporary) environmental design education where the societal responsibilities of future designers are often overshadowed by a focus on technical training.

At his time, Tomás Maldonado offered a parallel provocation, urging design professionals to act 'under the umbrella of the community as a homogeneous and morally monolithic pressure group, together with environmental scientists working not only on abstract models but on concrete solutions to real-world problems.'[70] In this spirit, I would like to invite fellow pedagogues to go beyond a depoliticised model of design education and actively pursue the integration of political awareness into our environmental teaching. If, as Beatriz Colomina puts it, 'protest has become pedagogy' in 1968, then perhaps today's pedagogy must become protest.[71]

Not only in service of society, but in response to the environmental crisis, an intersectional struggle binds human struggles to ecosystemic ones. In this context, we need a pedagogy of 'academic quest and endemic unrest',[72] one that acknowledges the designer's role as a political actor within complex, interdependent ecosystems. Far from the artificialising gaze of the *cadre de vie,* psychologist Monique Eleb described that frame of life at the Institut de l'Environnement as seeking to contain and manage the environment through design. What emerges instead is a need to embrace the messiness, the entanglement, the instability of our contemporary world. Rather than framing, bounding or simplifying our roles as pedagogues and practitioners, it may be possible to reserve space for complexity, to refuse neat solutions, to imagine otherwise and to nurture a culture of learning that is adaptive, situated, embodied and alive.

Elena Falomo

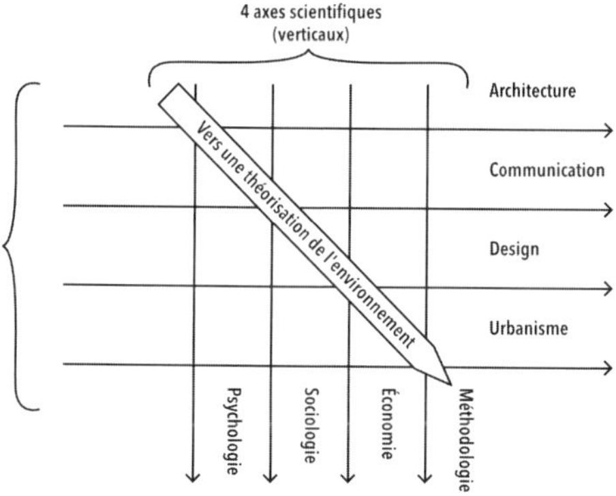

● Scheme of the goals of the Institut de l'Environnement.

● Collage attached to Marie Madeleine Michel's thesis.

EDUCATING GODS: DESIGN PEDAGOGY, DOMES AND THE PARADOX OF SEALED UTOPIAS

In 1968, amid ecological awakening and Cold War tension, students barricaded the streets of Paris demanding revolution, and 22 April 1970 saw the first Earth Day demonstration in the United States. However, another upheaval unfolded in design schools. Here, architects and designers turned their gaze upward—to outer space, the last blank canvas for their design vision. A vacuum hostile to life became the testing ground for hermetically sealed utopias where rationalist design could simulate 'perfect' worlds even as Earth's own ecosystems faltered.

'We *are* as gods and might as well get used to it',[73] declared Stewart Brand in the first edition of the *Whole Earth Catalog* in the fall of 1968 capturing this techno-utopian impulse. But as geodesic domes[74] sprouted in NASA labs and director Douglas Trumbull's film *Silent Running* (1972) haunted cinemas with its dying biospheres, the question became more pressing: were these space-age utopias meant to be blueprints for salvation, or were they just design hubris dressed in aluminium alloys?

There was a deep-rooted faith behind such visions. After World War II, scientific advancements—both medical and technological—brought the Western average citizens dramatic improvements in quality of life, strengthening their faith in rational solutions. Ironically, this very rationalism turned into a double-edged sword during the Cold War. The scientific mindset that had been improving the quality of life in the West turned out to also be the source of the fears of nuclear annihilation and ecological collapse that permeated the cultural zeitgeist at the time. The scientific mindset was simultaneously hailed as the omnipotent saviour from these existential threats which it created.

The directors of institutions like the Hochschule für Design Ulm (HfG Ulm), the Bauhaus and the Institut de l'Environnement (IE) had embraced scientific rationalism and the corresponding principles of pedagogy themselves. The heads of HfG and IE had created intellectual bubbles in which Bauhaus traditions merged with cybernetics and systems thinking—blending design, science and fiction. In this context, former HfG Ulm teacher and IE co-founder Claude Schnaidt argued that rationalist education meant teaching students to 'measure, calculate and analyse ... instilling a sense of reality.'[75] According to the teachings of cybernetics, global problems were quantifiable puzzles awaiting logical solutions—a belief that included the idea that design was a means to unveil the world's hidden truths.

Yet, even as designers and classrooms embraced cybernetics, cracks emerged. In her book *Silent Spring* (1962), Rachel Carson had revealed that the scientific solutions designed to kill pests also poisoned soil, wildlife and people. This book put forward that the fatal flaw of cybernetics and design rationalism was their insistence on reality being quantifiable in its totality—and thus controllable. *Silent Spring* showcased Earth as a messy assemblage of unquantifiable connections that defied calculation, and as

● Alain Leloup giving a lecture at the Institut de l'Environnement.

● Costas Iconomou's thesis *Entopia,* Paris, 1971.

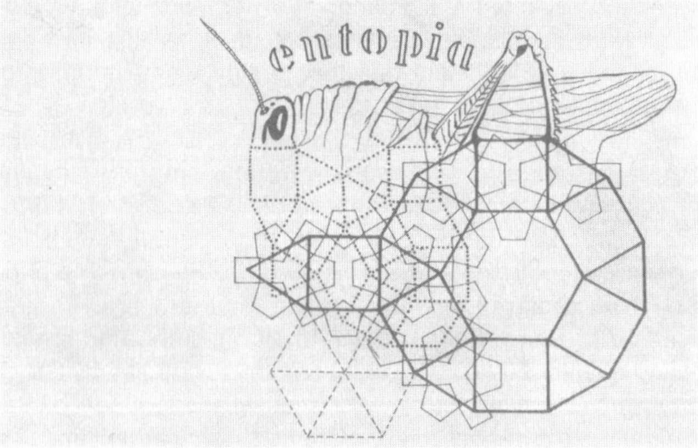

Karen Barad, an American feminist theorist and physicist, warns, we must be 'attentive to what gets excluded as well as what comes to matter.'[76]

Outer space, by its very nature, appeared to offer designers an escape from this dilemma: a sterile void in which every parameter could, in theory, be dictated, where rationalism could reign unchallenged by Earth's messy assemblage.

Space is a vacuum, an environment that is completely inhospitable and hostile to all life forms, a perfect blank canvas for the imagination of storytellers where only human ingenuity, self-reliance and technology would prevail. It also serves as a perfect playing field for utopian visions of architecture—a playing field on which architecture and design can, and should, create a fully controlled environment in its own right. A vision of architecture which hermetically separates the outside world from the architect's meticulously designed 'perfect' conditions, crafted by the one who knows best: the architect and designer—pure architectural hubris.

This vision of space as a sterile void—where architects could dictate 'perfect' conditions untethered by Earth's chaos—was not merely speculative. It mirrored a growing desperation back on Earth where the effects of industrial capitalism rendered terrestrial environments increasingly hostile to human survival. The photograph 'Blue Marble' (1972) presented the public with an image of Earth floating in infinite darkness, a fragile biosphere under siege, echoing Buckminster Fuller's 'spaceship Earth' metaphor.[77] If Earth was a vessel with finite resources, Fuller argued, then architecture had to function like a closed-loop lifeboat—a concept that resonated with the era's environmental and countercultural movements.

The hippie embrace of geodesic domes epitomised this shift. Communes like Drop City in Colorado (1965) and research initiatives like The Farallones Institute in California (1969) did not just adopt Fuller's domes as cheap housing—they saw them as proto-ecological arks, blending space-age aesthetics with back-to-the-land survivalism. The geodesic dome became a tool for probing the perils and possibilities of the geological epoch we now refer to as the Anthropocene.

Yet this idealism collided with reality as Fuller's technocratic precision clashed with the chaotic self-sufficiency of eco-communities. The sci-fi film *Silent Running* laid bare the paradox of engineered survival. Set aboard the *Valley Forge,* a spaceship preserving Earth's last ecosystems in geodesic domes after planetary collapse, the film demonstrates that these sealed environments could simulate life but never replicate its messy interdependence. You can engineer oxygen levels, but not grief.

Freeman Lowell, the ship's botanist and lone eco-activist, embodies this crisis. In a moment of desperate clarity, he cries, 'We're not meant to play god. But we have to, because nobody else is going to', reflecting Brand's opening statement in the *Whole Earth Catalog*. The film's dying space biospheres mirrored real-world failures—from overheated commune domes to the New Alchemy Institute's struggles to balance technology with ecology.

● The image depicts the Climatron, a geodesic dome greenhouse, at the Missouri Botanical Garden in 1960. It was the world's first completely air-conditioned greenhouse and the first geodesic dome to be enclosed in rigid Plexiglass panels. Library of Congress, Historic American Buildings Survey.

These sealed life support bubbles couldn't account for the unquantifiable and messy assemblages that made Earth's systems resilient. As Karen Barad might argue, the domes' exclusion of soil microbes, storms and social strife revealed the hubris of 'sealed' design. The geodesic dome endures as a symbol of this era's contradictions—a shape that contained both the arrogance of human mastery and the desperation of a species fighting for survival. In NASA's labs, it promised a sterile future; in hippie communes, it became a squat in the Anthropocene.

● View of Drop City, 'The Complex', in El Moro outside Trinidad, Colorado, c. 1966, photo: Clark Richert.

Silent Running's dead biospheres and Carson's poisoned soil asked the same unanswerable question: can you engineer a world that excludes life's uncontrollable excess—its grief, its rot, its wildness—and still call it living?

The 1960s dreamed of space as a blank slate, but Earth had already been written over too many times. What remains is Brand's unanswered challenge, 'We are as gods.' The domes—rusted in deserts, fetishised in tech hubs—remind us that gods, too, must reckon with the dirt under their nails.

Felix Bell

A man carrying a large TV on the cover of Victor Papanek's *Design for the Real World,* 1971.

The same man carrying the Paris Institute. IE Nanterre. *Bulletin d'informations inter-etablissement,* 1975.

AN INSTITUTE FOR THE REAL WORLD?

The Institut de l'Environnement (IE) aimed to train a new type of teacher: a pluridisciplinary designer who could find their way in other fields and thereby improve the shaping of the built environment through education. The knowledge produced in the institute's box with its modular façade was sometimes deemed too avant-garde to be used in real life. For instance, the institute had made some of the most advanced computers of its time available to the *stagiaires,* but these surpassed by far what any other organisation could provide if the IE's former students started working there. The knowledge of how to use the computers became nearly impossible to apply.

Only a few years after the institute's dissolution in 1971 in Paris, which marked the end of Claude Schnaidt's association with it, the new institute, now located in Nanterre, published a satirical image of a poor man carrying the industrial building of the Paris institute on his back. The photograph is identical to the one on the cover of the 1972 edition of Victor Papanek's *Design for the real world*[78] in which the same man carries an excessively large TV, its design clearly not suited to the needs of this 'real-world human'. The Institut de l'Environnement was inspired by systems striving to create a pedagogy based on interconnected elements forming a system that may be understood as a whole. In the case of the IE, different disciplines worked together, creating a process which resulted in formulating a theory for the environment. At the same time, it wanted to be connected to the real world, to understand design as the main factor that shapes our environment and is therefore more important than other disciplines. But the satirical image from Nanterre questions and critiques whether the original institute was any use at all to the real world it wanted to change so badly.

The IE's ideals stemmed from the principles of bringing functionality back into the human surroundings. Jean Baudrillard, the famous philosopher who came to give lectures at the institute, states that the Bauhaus brought about a system of functionalist signification in design. This means that by arguing that function was paramount, the Bauhaus made the interpretation of an object more important than the object itself.[79] In theory, this reduces complexity: everything has its function, and everything is rational. The Institut de l'Environnement continued this tradition in its own way. With their aim to integrate the design and theorisation of the built environment into other disciplines and create new ways of teaching this, the environment itself becomes a system, and its signification is to be shaped and attributed by the designer.

In the episode 'Le malentendu du design' (The misunderstanding of design) from the TV series *Vivre Aujourd'hui* presented by Jacques Frémontier, Jean-Pierre Grunfeld, who would later be recruited to teach at the IE thanks to this television appearance, criticises all the kitsch around him.[80] He pleads for designers to intervene in the real world and says, 'Currently, design is everything and nothing.' And pointing to the columns in the street he states that 'there are persistent signs, and then there is the reality which is here. There is all this, all these colours, all these shapes, these extraordinary things like the columns of the subway. What is wrong is not the column itself; it is the Greek column. Why is a Greek column supporting the subway?' Grunfeld implores designers to create objects and settings for our built environment with more consideration for their meanings and implications instead of making everything with 'fake shameful plastic' out of convenience or staying stuck in images from the past.

A little over 50 years after the Institut de l'Environnement, the Bauhaus Lab 2024 started investigating the IE with a team of eight young multidisciplinary researchers, curators, designers, architects and teachers. We created an exhibition whose three thematic parts interrelate and tell the institute's story, supplemented by interview videos. We aimed to tell the story of the IE from our point of view by highlighting the cultural context (outside), its pedagogical activities (inside) and the façade (as a membrane in-between). In the process of conceptualising this, we often noticed how the Bauhaus Lab format replicated the IE's methods in its pluridisciplinary and experimental ways.

In less sarcastic words than Grunfeld's, Abraham Moles wrote in the Institut de l'Environnement's journal that 'the designer appears as the god of relations between man and society',[81] an agent in the system working for the optimisation of human living conditions. Although I strongly disagree with ascribing such a divine role to the designer, it has been difficult for me (defining myself as a design researcher) to distance myself from a wish to create systems to communicate meaning. To a certain extent, one could see the presentation of the Bauhaus Lab, the exhibition enclosed in a space filled with connected elements, as a system too. The moment when we designed our structural elements and defined their relationships was the moment I understood our research more fully. Once again, the system and the signification of its elements were back, but this time I was there to experience the process.

The exhibition made the somewhat indirect connection between the Bauhaus school and the institute explicit in a new form. Having been a source of inspiration for the IE's ideals before, now, in our exhibition, the Bauhaus physically surrounded every aspect of the story we told about the institute. To make this connection even more obvious, we even branded the Bauhaus's glass curtain façade with signage reading 'Institut de l'Environnement', playing with the idea of layering these pedagogies. I would have loved to ask Baudrillard what he thought about this signification!

While reading up on the IE, I found the coldness of systems and their lack of playfulness uninspiring and difficult to deal with. Abraham Moles wrote, 'The environment *acts* on man who *reacts* to it forming a feedback loop *(Rückkopplung)* where the being becomes conscious of himself through the image of his actions that the surrounding world sends back to him as a sort of *mirror.*' [82] Again, Moles simplifies too much for my taste, but perhaps, the looking-glass he mentions is the way to escape from it. In the exhibition, this mirror is literally present: the table where visitors can contribute to the IE's narrative by depicting what environment means to them on a piece of paper, features a mirrored window, reflecting the viewer into the exhibition, into the environment, into history.

This reflection became a vital element. In his mysterious thesis, Costas Iconomou, a *stagiaire* at the IE, wrote, 'Every system appears like the reign of a world of shining seashells, but empty of their living organisms.' [83] The table with the mirror opened up the system, made it participatory and allowed these living creatures back in. Even if only symbolically, it opened a window into the visitors' creativity that we could not have predicted. The contributions which then were hung up on the other side of the document curtain ranged from a drawing of McDonald's to interpretations of the Bauhaus Building as a 'Boobhaus' or 'Baumhaus' to colourful squiggles and lines, landscapes full of vegetation, religious symbols, self-portraits and underwater creatures now bringing life to the 'shell' we created.

● Bringing life into systems—a page from Costas Iconomou's thesis *Entopia,* 1971.

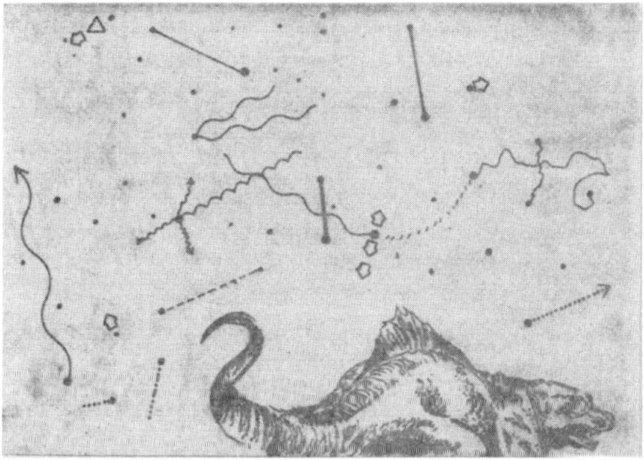

● Some of the contributions by visitors of the Bauhaus Lab 2024 exhibition.

I realise I cannot answer my initial question about the adequacy of the IE's knowledge for the 'real world.' It is a world I have only experienced through typewriter pages tucked in folders still carrying the smell of cigarettes. However, I can look back at our exhibition and see the importance of one thing: while we created a system that was relevant to us to make sense of research materials, we also allowed a bit of surrealism to enter, playing upon 'the distance instituted by the functionalist calculus between the object and itself, or between man and his own body, upon the distance between any term and the abstract finality that is imposed upon it.'[84] So here is my recommendation for creating something using a systems approach, whether for education or understanding something better: don't forget to leave enough space, and invite the (sur)real world to come in.

Louise Mazet

‘That seems to me to be the basis of teaching: learning to listen to each other in our differences and to bring together something that is obviously collective, which is the environment, where we live, what we share.’

Gérard Paris-Clavel in conversation with Bauhaus Lab members, 2024

INTERVIEW WITH GÉRARD PARIS-CLAVEL (B. 1943), FORMER STAGIAIRE

23 July 2024, Paris | abridged transcript

● Gérard Paris-Clavel.

[Bauhaus Lab]
Can you please tell us who you are and how you encountered the Institut de l'Environnement?

[Paris-Clavel]
I'm a graphic designer, and I studied for two years as a *stagiaire* at the institute. My fellows (i.e. the graphic design collective Grapus) and I were no longer students when we joined the institute; we had already done our studies and were part of a generation which was brought up with the Algerian War, big social movements and the Vietnam War.
I initially studied at a School of Applied Art in Paris, and then I went with Pierre Bernard and other friends to the Arts Academy in Warsaw where I began to discover intellectuality in my work. With the events of 1968, we ended up at the École des Arts Déco, discovering collective work in the 'Ateliers Populaires', reflecting on the way to inscribe images in political struggles anonymously. In 69, from the École des Arts Déco, I came to the institute which enabled me and my peers to work a lot with words, through reflections and in a collective manner, and that suddenly enabled us to start theorising our practices. And above all, to work.
Before the institute, we'd never discussed with architects, designers and very rarely with photographers. Schnaidt's attempt was precisely to create a collective based on this notion of environment, to see how singular disciplines could work together on the topic of the city.
The institute lasted only two years, it should have had to last five to ten years to fulfil its objective of training teachers, which wasn't the case because our diplomas weren't recog-

nized as teachers' ones. The inner dynamic of teaching and research at the institute was intended also for *stagiaires* producing pedagogical materials and knowledge that benefitted future generations of *stagiaires,* for example, through thesis work.

[Bauhaus Lab]
Can you describe the atmosphere at the institute?

[Paris-Clavel]
As a student we're all fresh out of 68, we were young, we were in great shape, and I remember a happy festive atmosphere. We were in a dynamic of upward movement, through political fights things were moving. We were a group, we were friends, we were always at a game or party. I didn't go to university before I joined the institute, so I didn't understand anything at all, but I was interested in it because of my friends and the dynamics.
There were very big fights, pretty violent, with heated discussions, but nonetheless for us it was a discovery. Whilst joining the institute, I was in the process of setting up François Pierre Grapus. We didn't have any money, but we've got vitality, an ironclad vitality, carried along by the 68 movement. We continued the movement artistically. In this period, we were discovering this notion of the collective that was very dear to Claude Schnaidt.

[Bauhaus Lab]
In our research we come across the idea of the transdisciplinary utopia that was the institute. How did you perceive this ideal?

[Paris-Clavel]
The relationships I remember the most were with my group of friends, Moreau, the communication design students. We were almost all graphic designers, we knew each other, we had studied together. I think we were definitely the group that was the least multidisciplinary group. We were always open to learning and to relationships, but our differences in political ideas may have prevented us from working on joint projects. We also came from different social backgrounds. We, as communist students, were isolated within the institute and constantly being criticised, which brought us closer together and distanced us from other groups. So for us, it was more the contribution of the teachers who taught us subjects we didn't have access to before. The proof is that all the research we did was among ourselves, all my research work was with collaborators I already knew.
You also have to realise that for us to get there was unique. Imagine a big building full of money, full of resources. It was unique.

[Bauhaus Lab]
Can you tell us more about the relationship with teachers?

[Paris-Clavel]
At the institute we were all interested in studying to transform the world. We were all militants, and it was a great movement. Therefore the relationship with the teachers was formidable, Claude Schnaidt was a marvellous person. We had an exceptional body of teachers. This also contributed to the fact that other schools started to begrudge the institute, be-

cause we were stealing their resources to feed the institute. It was exceptional conditions, it was a serious instrument of play, and above all, I think it was a special atmosphere.
There weren't big age differences between the teachers and the students: five to ten years age difference at most, and all the teachers were progressive. There was a political dynamic, a common desire to work to transform the world, even if it sounds pretentious to say, to transform the city, to transform things, so we were really interested in the complexities that we were exploring.
Teachers really had this desire not to look down on someone to whom they passed on their knowledge, they would encourage them to read. I think I'm a good example of someone who arrived without any knowledge and who benefited from their generosity in sharing. I remember the pleasure I had talking and discussing with Eisenbeis, Schnaidt, Haumont ... It was always enjoyable because they revealed things to us. They were people who coated you with layers of knowledge, meaning that they make you feel like you're not stupid around them, because they actually teach you things by talking to you, and that's what was so powerful. They don't just give you knowledge, they teach you what you know but haven't had the means to express or reveal. Suddenly you realise you have it, but they brought it out in you.

[Bauhaus Lab]
At the Institut de l'Environnement, how did you talk about the concept of the environment? What did the concept of the environment mean to you?

[Paris-Clavel]
For me, it was the forms of everyday life. They understood that environmental design is in everyday life, in the most familiar use, that a population finds the qualities of forms. You see, that's what we found interesting. It wasn't about working on the excellence of masterpieces, it was about working on architecture, the city, housing, visual communication .... Schnaidt didn't see visual communication as advertising, he didn't see it as graphic design, he didn't even see it as we saw it as political communication, he saw it in identification systems, networks, brands, social systems ...

[Bauhaus Lab]
And did your experience at the institute influence your work with the Grapus collective afterwards?

[Paris-Clavel]
Of course, because we were still in a country that was very much still dominated by narrow corporatism. The institute allowed us, in professional terms, to gather knowledge. We were better equipped than others in the profession, we found it easier to talk to clients about the subject matter than others who were just responding to an order with a production. Whereas after the institute, we had this notion of context and circumstances, of supporting the work, and finally ... we were part of a collective, which meant that people had enormous strength because there were several of us working on the same subject, so inevitably there was more knowledge being shared and therefore more rich material. The institute brought us to a level that we would never have had in the French education system.

[Bauhaus Lab]
How did you experience the dissolution of the institute?

[Paris-Clavel]
We were unhappy because we had really invested in it. We fought for our diplomas, not just to have a diploma. We already had plenty of diplomas, but the Institute's one would have given us a status that would have allowed us to teach at a recognised level with a salary. We also wanted to teach teachers because there was a big lack at the time in the quality of teaching. There was no teacher training in our subjects, so it would have allowed us, through the connection with the institute, to transmit that knowledge.
You can see it clearly after the institute, how things turned out. The architects took over the thick stuff, we did little things that didn't work, and then the schools changed.

[Bauhaus Lab]
In your opinion, were the internal contradictions you mentioned also at the root of the closure of the institute?

[Paris-Clavel]
It was the whole cultural sector which made it impossible for many schools to get loans. Schools didn't have much of a budget, and what little budget there was it went to the institute. It was thanks to Malraux that the opening of the institute was possible at the time. It's clear that the people who came after him were more reactionary people in the government who saw themselves as not left-wing. We were labelled communists, they said the institute wanted to form dangerous so-

ciety destroyers, the school was expensive, etc. So they also used the excuse of the leftists who did break things, who did damage the school. It was a pretext for the government to stop the experiment. At the same time there was no relay; it wasn't really understood by other universities. The multidisciplinary attitude was still contrary to what was happening at the time with the mandarins and the hierarchical order, so I think that contributed as well.

[Bauhaus Lab]
Which lessons can we learn from the Institut de l'Environnement?

[Paris-Clavel]
It was a fundamental thing in France, in my opinion, because it allowed groups like us and many others, even in architecture, to understand. When you look at the texts, the programmes, ... there are still things we could draw inspiration from to improve the current situation in many schools or academies.
We can't say it was a failure. It's still an experience that has fed into other things, so we feel that it's less powerful because the period is different, but it was still part of a movement. It created a path. And we could imagine that one day we could recreate a place where there is a training programme for teacher-researchers, which is the training of teachers in our disciplines, based on the idea of working with others and creating a collective. That seems to me to be the basis of teaching: learning to listen to each other in our differences and to bring together something that is obviously collective, which is the environment, where we live, what we share.

Appendix

- *Rafael Amato* is a graphic designer and design historian with a degree in Design from the Federal University of Minas Gerais and a Master's in Theory and History of Design from the Faculty of Architecture and Urbanism at the University of São Paulo (FAU USP), both in Brazil. His research focuses on Latin American modernisms, design education and transnational design dialogues, conflicts and encounters.

- *Felix Bell* is a spatial designer and object maker whose work reflects on the tension between designs' anthropic origins and our inherent animality. Holding a Master's degree in Geo-Design from the Design Academy Eindhove, Netherlands, he often embraces transdisciplinary design-research to tell stories focused on bridging the engrained divides that exist between culture and nature by giving agency to the invisible or unnoticed relationships between non-human beings to whom we are bound in modern life.

- *Elena Falomo* is a designer whose practice inhabits art, research, design and pedagogy, exploring social and ecological questions through collaborative processes. She holds a double Master's in Innovation Design Engineering from the Royal College of Art and Imperial College London, UK. She is the co-founder of the Living Summer School and a pedagogue active in universities across Europe.

- *Or Haklai* is an architect and design researcher focusing on critical approaches across art, architecture and urban theory. She holds a BArch from Bezalel Academy of Arts and Design, Jerusalem, Israel, (2018) and an MA in the cultural studies programme from the Hebrew University of Jerusalem (2023). Her latest study examined the city of Tel Aviv and the Azrieli Center skyscrapers project as a symbol of the shift toward a global city.

- *Teresa Häußler* is an exhibition designer, scenographer and curatorial researcher based in Berlin, Germany. She explores connections between space, politics and representation. Her current practice evolves around questions of display, examining different layers of history and deconstructing narratives of modernity. She graduated from Karlsruhe University of Arts and Design in 2023.

- *Louise Mazet* is a design researcher with a background in communication, media and philosophy. She has a Master's degree in Gendering Practices from the University of Gothenburg, Sweden, and a second one in Design Research from Anhalt University of Applied Sciences, Dessau, in collaboration with the Bauhaus Dessau Foundation. She is currently a PhD candidate at Hasselt University, Belgium, focusing on the possibilities of living labs as participatory feminist utopias.

- *María Paszkiewicz* is an architect and independent curator, holding a Master's degree in Curatorial Studies from the University of Navarra, Spain, and a Master's degree in History of Architecture from Torcuato Di Tella University, Buenos Aires, Argentina (2019). As a professor, she teaches architectural history and theory as well as Latin American art history. Currently, she is pursuing an international PhD between the University of Navarra and the

Karlsruhe Institute of Technology (KIT), Germany, focusing on pedagogical exchanges and methodologies in design and architecture education.

● *Jie Shen* is a PhD candidate in architectural history at the University of Tokyo, Japan, and was a visiting research fellow at TU Darmstadt, Germany (2023–2024). Her research explores the intersections of architectural history, science and technology studies, and development theory, with a focus on narratives of modernisation, industrialisation, mechanisation and labour in the Global South. Her dissertation examines the transfer of construction knowledge between China and regions within and beyond the socialist bloc during the Cold War, centring on the history of cranes. Trained as an architect, she previously worked on heritage conservation and public building projects in China. Her research work has been supported by the Obayashi Foundation, the Society of Architectural Historians and the SOM Foundation, among others.

● Bauhaus Lab members, 2024.

● Bauhaus Taschenbuch 30
The book was published in the context of the Bauhaus Lab 2024 exhibition presented at the Bauhaus Dessau from 09 August 2024 to 21 April 2025.

● Edited by
Bauhaus Dessau Foundation
Director Dr Barbara Steiner
Gropiusallee 38
06846 Dessau-Roßlau
Telephone +49-340-6508-250
www.bauhaus-dessau.de

● Academy Team, Bauhaus Dessau Foundation:
Programme head: Dr Regina Bittner
Research associate: Philipp Sack

● Bauhaus Lab 2024 participants:
Rafael Amato, Felix Bell, Elena Falomo, Or Haklai, Teresa Häußler, Louise Mazet, María Paszkiewicz, Jie Shen

● Editing
Petra Frese

● Translation and Copyediting
Bauhaus Lab 2024
Petra Frese, Rebecca Philipps Williams

● Project management
Katja Klaus, Jie Shen

● Graphic design
Anne Meyer
based on a concept by HORT, Berlin
www.hort.org.uk

● Printed by
Pöge Druck, Leipzig
www.poegedruck.de

● Publisher
Spector Books Verlagsgesellschaft mbh, Leipzig
www.spectorbooks.com

● Distribution
Germany, Austria: GVA, Gemeinsame Verlagsauslieferung Göttingen GmbH & Co. KG,
www.gva-verlage.de
Switzerland: AVA Verlagsauslieferung AG, www.ava.ch
France, Belgium: Interart Paris, www.interart.fr
UK: Central Books Ltd, www.centralbooks.com
USA, Canada, Central and South America, Africa: ARTBOOK | D.A.P. www.artbook.com
Japan: twelvebooks, www.twelve-books.com
South Korea: The Book Society, www.thebooksociety.org
Australia, New Zealand: Perimeter Distribution,
www.perimeterdistribution.com

The Bauhaus Dessau Foundation is a non-profit foundation under public law. It is institutionally funded by:

Der Beauftragte der Bundesregierung für Kultur und Medien

SACHSEN-ANHALT

Dessau
Roßlau

First edition, 2025

ISBN 978-3-95905-918-3

● Front page
Alain Leloup, 1970

● Exhibition photos p. 35–50
Bauhaus Dessau Foundation.

p. 38–39 | 45 Felix Bell

p. 40–43 | 46–51 Thomas Meyer

p. 44 María Paszkiewicz

1 Claude Schnaidt. *Umweltbürger und Umweltmacher,* Dresden: Verlag der Kunst, 1982.
2 Tomás Maldonado. *Umwelt und Revolte. Zur Dialektik des Entwerfens im Spätkapitalismus,* Reinbek bei Hamburg: Rowohlt, 1972.
3 Simon Sadler. 'Mandalas or raised fists? Hippie holism, Panther totality and another modernism', in: Andrew Blauvelt (ed.). Hippie modernism. *The struggle for Utopia,* Minneapolis, Minnesota: Walker Art Center, 2015, p. 117.
4 Torsten Lange. *Komplexe Umweltgestaltung. Architectural theory and the production of the built environment in the German Democratic Republic* (GDR) 1960–1990. PhD thesis, vol. 1. University College London, https://www.google.com/url?sa=t&source=web&rct=-j&opi=89978449&url=https://discovery.ucl.ac.uk/id/eprint/1471552/19/2015_10_03_KUG_Lange_PhD-thesis_vol-I.pdf&ved=2ahUKEwik6I7tzt-OAxV16wIHHS-biDHwQFnoECBkQAQ&usg=AOvVaw0WafqbdQy-gAsHUrjuMd3DE (accessed 27.5.2025)
5 Tony Côme. *L'Institut de l'Environnement: Une école décloisonnée,* Paris: Éditions B42, 2017.
6 On 6 and 7 June 2024, Bauhaus Lab members visited the gta Archive's collection on Claude Schnaidt.
7 Peter Sulzer. *Jean Prouvé—Complete works: Volume 4: 1954–1984,* Basel: Birkhäuser, 2008, pp. 141, 142, 146.
8 Documents on the Bâtiment rue Èrasme PARIS 5°, DEVIS DESCRIPTIF & ESTIMATIF SOMMAIRES, in the gta Archive on Claude Schnaidt, 187-4-2-17 IE Photos/bâtiment.
9 Aleyda Resendiz-Vazquez. *L'industrialisation du bâti-*

ment: Le cas de la préfabrication dans la construction scolaire en France (1951–1973), PhD thesis, Conservatoire national des arts et metiers-CNAM, 2010, https://theses.hal.science/tel-00554230/ (accessed 7 July 2025).

10 Adrian Leander Pöllinger. *Jean Prouvé: Experimentelle Schulbauten 1931–1974,* PhD thesis, ETH Zurich, 2021, https://www.research-collection.ethz.ch/handle/20.500 11850/486761 (accessed 7 July 2025).

11 Sulzer, p. 248.

12 Ibid., p. 143.

13 Robert Joly was commissioned as the architect of the Institut de l'Environnement by the Minister of Cultural Affairs, André Malraux, in 1968.

14 Adrian Leander Pöllinger. 'Open systems for open plans: Jean Prouvé's contribution to school building systems in the 1960s and 1970s', in: *History of construction cultures, volume 2,* Boca Raton, Florida: CRC Press, 2021, pp. 751–757, https://www.taylorfrancis.com/chapters/oa-edit/10.1201/9781003173434-210/open-systems-open-plans-jean-prouv%C3%A9-contribution-school-building-systems-1960s-1970s-leander-p%C3%B6llinger (accessed 7 July 2025).

15 Ibid.

16 Tony Côme, Andrés Ávila Gómez, Diana Carolina Ruiz. 'De la Hochschule für Gestaltung de Ulm al Institut de l'Environnement de París: Revoluciones en la enseñanza de la arquitectura y el diseño durante los años 1960', in: *Apuntes: Revista de estudios sobre patrimonio cultural,* 31, no. 2 (2018), https://doi.org/10.11144/Javeriana.apc31-2.hgui (accessed 7 July 2025).

17 In an Interview with Akiko Takehara by Bauhaus Lab members on 24 July 2024 in Paris.

18 *Environnement* 1, Paris: Institut de l'Environnement, 1971.

19 Claude Schnaidt. 'Claude Cobbi—allocution faite au cimetière du Montparnasse le 19 mai 1995', *in: Autrement dit: écrits 1950–2001,* Gollion: Infolio, 2004, p. 268.

20 Arlette Farge. *The allure of the archives,* New Haven: Yale University Press, 2013, p. 78.

21 Arlette Farge. *Lugares para a história,* Belo Horizonte: Autêntica Editora, 2015, p. 71.

22 Marc Bloch. *The historian's craft,* Manchester: Manchester University Press, 1992.

23 I would like to draw attention in particularly to the 'Statement made by the French group' (1970) by Jean Baudrillard in Aspen, which offered a radical interpretation of the relationship between design and the environment. The group believed that this relationship could distract citizens from other crucial social and political issues. See: Jean Aubert and Jean Baudrillard. 'The environmental witchhunt. Statement by the French group, 1970', in: Reyner Banham (ed.). *The Aspen papers: Twenty years of design theory from the International Design Conference in Aspen,* London: Praeger, 1974, pp. 208–210.

24 Tony Côme dedicated himself to researching the IE, which resulted in the book *L'Institut de l'environnement: une école décloisonnée.* In a conversation with us during the Bauhaus Lab in May 2024, Côme pointed out that even within the French context, he is often asked why he chose to research such an institute. See Tony Côme.

L'Institut de l'environnement: une école décloisonnée. Urbanisme, architecture, design, communication, Montreuil: Éditions B42, 2017.

25 Max Bill, *Letter addressed to Claude Schnaidt* (HfG-Archiv, AZS 0090 Korrespondenz HfG 1954–1970 Claude Schnaidt, February 1956).

26 Claude Schnaidt. 'Prefabricated hope', in: *ulm* 10/11 (1964), pp. 2–9.

27 Claude Schnaidt. 'Architecture and political commitment', in: *ulm* 19/20 (1967), pp. 29–34.

28 For a better understanding of this debate, see: Rafael Amato, Teresa Häußler. 'Institut de l'environnement—A radical reinterpretation of the Ulm model', in: Chris Dähne, Helge Svenshon, Martin Mäntele (eds.). *Programmed for hope. Architectural experimentation at the HfG Ulm building department,* Stuttgart: av edition GmbH, 2025, pp. 127–139.

29 Philippe Artières. 'Arquivar a própria vida', in: *Revista estudos históricos* 11, no. 21 (1998), p. 31.

30 In a text written in 1972, Schnaidt describes the IE's dissolution as a result of a precarious existence, see: Claude Schnaidt. 'Epilog einer makabren Geschichte über die Umwelt', in: *Umweltbürger und Umweltmacher,* Dresden: Verlag der Kunst, 1982, pp. 295–299.

31 Umberto Eco. *Semiotics and the philosophy of language,* Bloomington: Indiana University Press, 1986, p. 59.

32 Robert Venturi, Denise Scott Brown, Steven Izenour. *Learning from Las Vegas: The forgotten symbolism of architectural form,* Cambridge, Massachusetts: MIT Press, 1977.

33 Tomás Maldonado. *Umwelt und Revolte. Zur Dialektik des Entwerfens im Spätkapitalismus,* Reinbek bei Hamburg: Rowohlt, 1972, p. 114.
34 Tony Côme, Institut de l'Environnement. 'Descendant du Bauhaus ou dernier bastion de mai 68?', in: *French Historical Studies,* 1 April 2018; 41 (2), p. 321.
35 Institut de l'Environnement. *Environnement* 1, Paris: Institut de l'Environnement, Feburary 1971.
36 Institut de l'Environnement. *Environnement* 2, Paris: Institut de l'Environnement, June 1971.
37 Maldonado, *Umwelt und Revolte,* p. 115.
38 Tom Holert. 'Ca. 1972': *Gewalt—Umwelt—Identität—Methode.* Leipzig: Spector Books, 2024.
39 Claude Schnaidt. 'Ausblick auf das zerklüftete Gelände der Umweltmacher und Umweltbürger', in: *Umweltmacher und Umweltbürger,* Dresden: Verlag der Kunst, 1982, pp. 302–311. The text is based on a lecture at the University of Geneva in 1972.
40 Claude Schnaidt. 'Die Umwelt und ihre Gestaltung', in: *Umweltmacher und Umweltbürger,* Dresden: Verlag der Kunst, 1982, p. 289.
41 Robert Spizzichino. 'Hypothèses pour une théorie de l'environnement', in: *Environnement* 2 (1971), p. 9.
42 Ibid., p. 8.
43 Horst W. J. Rittel and Melvin M. Webber. 'Dilemmas in a general theory of planning', in: *Policy Sciences,* 4 (1973), pp. 155–169, here p. 160. A modification of a paper presented to the panel on policy sciences, American Association for the Advancement of Science, Boston, December 1969.

44 Claude Schnaidt. 'Editorial', in: *Environnement* 1 (1970), p. 1.
45 Spizzichino, p. 1.
46 Maldonado. *Umwelt und Revolte.*
47 Term used by Simon Sadler on 22 May 2024 in conversation with Bauhaus Lab participants to describe the state of relative instability and contestation of the concept of the 'environment' at UC Berkeley towards the end of the 1960s that was partly taken over by the Institut de l'Environnement.
48 Akiko Takehara, former *staigiaire* at the IE, in conversation with Bauhaus Lab participants on 24 July 2024 in Paris.
49 Monique Ebb, Jeanne Quéheillard. 'The Institute of the Environment: the experience of a utopia (1969–1976)', in: ROSA B, 5 (2013), http://rosab.net/en/the-french-situation-relations/the-institut-of-environment-the.html?lang=en (accessed 10 June 2025).
50 Beatriz Colomina, *Radical pedagogies conference,* organised by the Center for Contemporary Architecture Studies and the Master's programme in history and criticism of architecture and the city, Torcuato Di Tella University, Buenos Aires, 2024, https://youtu.be/zE2-GPQ21wY?si=FYnTyGgSHEi21P (accessed 24 June 2025).
51 *L'Architecture d'Aujourd'hui: Nouvel Environnement* 145 (1969), p. V.
52 Claude Schnaidt. 'Editorial', in: *Environnement* 1 (1971), p. 1–2.
53 Maldonado. *Umwelt und Revolte.*

54 Joaquín Medina Warmburg. 'El mundo como artefacto. Tomás Maldonado en el foco del diseño ambiental (1966–1972)', in: *Revista de Arquitectura,* 2017, p. 25.
55 Maldonado was a professor at Princeton University (1967–1970) when he gave the lecture. Years earlier, Robert Geddes, Dean of Architecture at Princeton, had visited him at the HfG Ulm to discuss environmental design. Geddes later persuaded Maldonado to join Princeton where his seminars were more theoretical and critical compared to his practice-based approach at the HfG. See Joaquín Medina Warmburg. 'Methods of Environmental Design', in: Beatriz Colomina et al. (eds.). *Radical pedagogies,* Cambridge, Massachusetts: MIT Press, 2022, pp. 134–135.
56 Tomás Maldonado, lecture delivered on 25 May 1970 at the auditorium of the Institut de l'Environnement. Claude Schnaidt/gta Archive, ETH Zurich. Unless otherwise noted, subsequent quotations are drawn from this lecture.
57 Venice Architecture Biennale. *Intelligens. Natural. Artificial. Collective,* 2025. https://www.labiennale.org/en/news/biennale-architettura-2025-intelligens-natural-artificial-collective (accessed 3 July 2025).
58 Tomás Maldonado, 'Naturaleza und Gesellschaft', in: Martin Krampen and Horst Kächele (eds.). *Umwelt, Gestaltung und Persönlichkeit: Reflexionen 30 Jahre nach Gründung der Ulmer Hochschule für Gestaltung,* Hildesheim: Georg Olms Verlag, 1986, p. 171.
59 'Internalities', Spanish Pavilion at the 19th International Architecture Exhibition, Venice Biennale, 2025, curated by Roi Salgueiro and Manuel Bouzas, https://www.

youtube.com/watch?v=YWiy36U2rgI (accessed 3 July 2025).

60 Tomás Maldonado. 'How to fight complacency in design education', in: *Journal of the Ulm School for Design (HfG),* no. 17/18 (1966), pp. 14–20.

61 Beatriz Colomina et al. (eds.). *Radical pedagogies.*

62 This is also the subtitle of the book which Tony Côme dedicated to the Institut de l'Environnement, *L'Institut de l'environnement: une école décloisonnée. Urbanisme, architecture, design, communication,* Paris: Éditions B42, 2017.

63 Paulo Freire in *Pedagogy of the oppressed,* trans. Myra Bergman Ramos (New York: Continuum, 2000), formulates 'the distinction between systematic education, which can only be changed by political power, and educational projects, which should be carried out with the oppressed in the process of organizing them.'

64 Côme.

65 Conference *Navigating informal education.* Held at Bolwerk, Kortrijk, 5–6 September 2024.

66 Safe spaces are commonly understood as environments where individuals can express themselves without fear of being challenged, judged or harmed. In contrast, brave spaces emphasise the need for courageous and respectful dialogue in which participants are expected to engage in challenging conversations, take risks and confront discomfort as part of the learning process. Rather than eliminating conflict, brave spaces aim to navigate it constructively. See Brian Arao and Kristi Clemens. 'From safe spaces to brave spaces: A new way to frame

dialogue around diversity and social justice', in: Lisa M. Landreman (ed.). *The art of effective facilitation: Reflections from social justice educators,* Sterling, Virgina: Stylus Publishing, 2013.
67 Marie Madeleine Michel. 'L'abandon d'un environment ne respondent plus aux besoins de l'espace – les tentative de creation d'un nouveu environnement', Claude Schnaidt archive/gta Archive, ETH Zurich.
68 Dominique Spinetta. 'Critique de l'einsegnement de l'architecture—recherche d'un enseignement critique', Claude Schnaidt archive/gta Archive, ETH Zurich.
69 Lucy Suchman. 'Design', in: *Fieldsights,* Society for Cultural Anthropology, mid-2017, https://culanth.org/fieldsights/design (accessed 16 June 2025).
70 Tomás Maldonado. *Umwelt und Revolte.*
71 Colomina, *Radical pedagogies.*
72 Ivan Illich. *Deschooling society,* New York: Harper and Row, 1971, p. 51.
73 Stewart Brand. *Whole Earth Catalog,* fall 1968, Menlo Park, California: Portola Institute, 1968, p. 2.
74 Developed by Richard Buckminster Fuller, a geodesic dome is a thin-shell hemispherical structure based on a geodesic polyhedron.
75 Claude Schnaidt. Unité pédagogique d'architecture n° 1, Paris, 4, date unknown.
76 Karen Barad. 'Posthumanist performativity: Toward an understanding of how matter comes to matter', in: *Signs: Journal of Women in Culture and Society* 28, no. 3 (2003), p. 827.
77 Richard Buckminster Fuller. *Operating manual for space-*

ship Earth, Carbondale, Illinois: Southern Illinois University Press, 1969.

78 Victor Papanek. *Design for the real world,* London: Thames and Hudson, 1971.

79 Jean Baudrillard. *For a critique of the political economy of the sign.* St. Louis, Missouri: Telos Press, 1981.

80 'Le malentendu du design', from: *Vivre Aujourd'hui.* Office de Radiodiffusion-Télévision Française, 1970.

81 Abraham Moles. 'La théorie des systèmes fonctionnels comme cadre du design de l'environnement', in: *Environnement* 1 (1970), p. 35.

82 Moles, p. 30.

83 Costas Iconomou. *Entopia,* thesis, Institut de l'Environnement, 1971, section 15.

84 Baudrillard, p. 193.

- p. 18/19/20/21/24
© gta Archive/ETH Zurich, estate of Claude Schnaidt.

- p. 22 above
© HfG-Archiv

- p. 22 below
© Akiko Takehara

- p. 30/31
© HfG-Archiv, AZS 0218 Originale Drucksachen

- p. 54/55/58
© gta Archive/ETH Zurich, estate of Claude Schnaidt

- p. 62
© Or Haklai

- p. 66
© Bauhaus Lab members

- p. 76
Photo: Alain Leloup © gta Archive/ETH Zurich, estate of Claude Schnaidt

- p. 79
Photo: Wolfgang Siol, © HfG-Archiv

- p. 81
Spizzichino, Robert. 'Hypothèses pour une théorie de

l'environnement', in: *Environnement* 2 (1971): p. 6
© gta Archive/ETH Zurich (Claude Schnaidt)

● p. 82/83
Spizzichino, Robert. 'Hypothèses pour une théorie de l'environnement', in: *Environnement* 2 (1971): p. 7
© Archive/ETH Zurich (Claude Schnaidt)

● p. 85
Photo: Wolfgang Siol, © HfG-Archiv

● p. 88/91
© gta Archive/ETH Zurich, photo: Alain Leloup.

● p. 98
© Bauhaus Lab members

● p. 114/115
© gta Archive/ETH Zurich, estate of Claude Schnaidt, photo: Alain Leloup.

● p. 121
© gta Archive/ETH Zurich, estate of Claude Schnaidt

● p. 124
© gta Archive/ETH Zurich

● p. 127
picryl Public Domain Media

- p. 128/129/132/137

© gta Archive/ETH Zurich

- p. 138

© Bauhaus Dessau Foundation

- p. 142

© Bauhaus Lab members

- p. 155

© Bauhaus Dessau Foundation

- Bauhaus Taschenbuch 2

Architektur aus der Schuhbox.
Bat'as internationale Fabrikstädte

- Bauhaus Taschenbuch 3

Kibbuz und Bauhaus. Pioniere des Kollektivs

- Bauhaus Taschenbuch 5

Das Bauhausgebäude in Dessau/The Bauhaus Building in Dessau

- Bauhaus Taschenbuch 6

Vom Bauhaus nach Palästina.
Chanan Frenkel, Ricarda und Heinz Schwerin

- Bauhaus Taschenbuch 7

Die Siedlung Dessau-Törten 1926 bis 1931

- Bauhaus Taschenbuch 9

Die unsichtbare Bauhausstadt. Eine Spurensuche in Dessau

- Bauhaus Taschenbuch 11

Junges Design am Bauhaus Dessau

- Bauhaus Taschenbuch 12

Bauhaus Lab 2013. Architecture after Speculation

- Bauhaus Taschenbuch 14

Die Werkbundsiedlung Stuttgart Weissenhof

- Bauhaus Taschenbuch 16
Die Dessauer Bauhausbauten

- Bauhaus Taschenbuch 17
Junges Design in den Meisterhäusern

- Bauhaus Taschenbuch 19
Mobilitätsdesign

- Bauhaus Taschenbuch 20
Desk in Exile: A Bauhaus Object Traversing Different Modernities

- Bauhaus Taschenbuch 21
Bauhaus World Heritage Site

- Bauhaus Taschenbuch 22
Between Chairs. Design Pedagogies in Transcultural Dialogue

- Bauhaus Taschenbuch 23
The Art of Joining—Designing the Universal Connector

- Bauhaus Taschenbuch 24
Handle with Care: Unpacking a Bulky Table

- Bauhaus Taschenbuch 25
A Concrete for the 'Other Half'?

- Bauhaus Taschenbuch 26
Vegetation under Power. Heat! Breath! Growth!

- Bauhaus Taschenbuch 27
Doors of Learning. Microcosms of a Future South Africa

- Bauhaus Taschenbuch 28
Not a Penguin Pool. Echoes of More-than-Human Entanglements